Blockchain

The Complete Insider Guide to
Comprehensive Universe of this
Revolution Technology, with Effective
Steps on How Blockchain Applies in
Investing and Trading that
Tremendously Impact on the Business
World

along and must not be taken as commands or expert instructions. The readers are responsible for his/her own action after reading this book.

Adherence to applicable regulations and laws, including local, state, federal and international government business practices, professional licensing, advertising and other aspects of doing business in Canada, US or other jurisdictions is the solitary responsibility of reader and purchaser.

Neither the publisher nor the author assumes any liability or responsibility whatsoever on the behalf of reader or purchaser of this material. Any received signal of an organization or an individual is purely unintentional.

Book Description

The blockchain is a new revolution in the field of technology. This technology is in developmental stages; therefore, a number of people don't know about it. There are lots of hypes and questions surrounding about blockchain, bitcoin, and cryptocurrencies. As a result, numerous people have incomplete information of this transformative technology.

This book is designed to offer you maximum details about blockchain and cryptocurrencies. If you want good information about future, implication, and effects of blockchain technology, this can be a good book for you. After reading this book, you will be able to understand blockchain, bitcoin, and its uses. The book offers:

- What is blockchain? And An Overview and Uses of Blockchain
- Role of Blockchain in Economy and Financial Services

- Understand the Future of the Blockchain and its Impact on Industries
- Challenges for Blockchain Technology
- Basic Terminology of Blockchain and Financial Market
- A Guide for the Beginners to Advance Traders
- Strategies to Secure Information and Data with Blockchain

Read this book and explore the world of blockchain and its wonders for your life.

Table of Content

Introduction

Blockchain aka block chain is a regionalized, digitized and public ledger of cryptocurrency transactions. It is a consistently growing list of particular records known as blocks that are allied and secured with the use of cryptography. Every block contains a botch pointer as a secured link to a preceding block, transaction data, and a timestamp. Blockchains are innately resistant to modification of data. This openly distributed ledger can record transactions between 2 parties in a permanent and verifiable way. For the use of blockchain as a distributed ledger, it is managed by peer-to-peer network adhering to the protocol for authenticating new blocks. After recording, the data in each block can't be changed retroactively without changing the subsequent blocks that require the involvement of the majority of the network.

Completed blocks are added and recorded to blockchain in sequential order. It allows participants of the market to keep the track of all transactions involving digital currency without principal recordkeeping. Every node (a connected computer to blockchain network) get a copy of blockchain that is automatically downloaded.

It is actually developed as an accounting method for virtual currency known as Bitcoin. Blockchains aka DLT (distributed ledger technology) exists in a number of profitable applications. Currently, blockchain technology is used to verify transactions. Within digital currency, it is easy to digitize, insert and code practically every document into blockchain. It allows you to create an ineradicable record that can't be changed. Moreover, the authenticity of record is easy to verify with the use of whole community using blockchain instead of using a sole centralized authority.

Chapter 1 – What is blockchain?

Blockchain consists of blocks that record different transactions. Once you record your data in a block, it goes in the permanent database of the blockchain. After completion of a block, a new block is automatically generated. Blockchain has countless numbers of these blocks associated with each other in a chronological and linear order. This is just like links in a chain. Each block has a particular hash of the earlier block. The blockchain contains complete information about the address of different users and their respective balances from the beginning block to the currently completed block.

The purpose of blockchain was to record immutable transactions so that no one can't delete them. A particular procedure cryptography is used to add blocks in the blockchain to keep them meddle-proof. It is possible to distribute data, but no one can copy this data. The ever-growing size of blockchain can be a problem in the future because there may be issues of synchronization and storage.

Bitcoin and Blockchains

The main technological innovation Bitcoin is related to the blockchain. Bitcoin is not regulated by a principal authority. The users often dictate and validate the transactions after receiving money for services or goods. It eliminates the need for a 3rd party to store payment or record this procedure. Each completed transaction is recorded publicly in blocks and ultimately in the blockchain. After recording, it is verified and conveyed by other users of Bitcoin. Typically, a new block in the blockchain is appended to blockchain in every ten minutes, through the procedure of mining.

As per the protocol of Bitcoin, the database of blockchain is shared by all available nodes in the system. Upon linking the network, every connected computer get a copy of blockchain that has records. It serves as a proof of every executed transaction. It may thus offer insight into particular facts like the value of a particular address in old times. You can get access to the whole Bitcoin blockchain via Blockchain.info.

Important Extensions of the Blockchains

To utilize traditional banking as a correspondence, the blockchain is similar to the complete history of the transactions of a financial institution. Every block is treated as a solitary bank statement. Since it is a distributed database system; therefore, it serves as an electronic ledger. A blockchain has the ability to simplify operations of a business for everyone. For all these reasons, the stock exchanges and financial institutions are attracting toward this technology. Businesses in other fields like IOT (Internet of Things) devices, insurance, diamonds, and music are also interested in this technology. As per the suggestions of advocates, this kind of ledger system can be a good choice for voting systems, medical records, registration of vehicle and weapon by state governments, and confirm ownership of artwork or antiquities.

The DLT (distributed ledger technology) has potential to simplify current operations of the business. New models of blockchain have started to replace the insufficient and expensive payment and accounting networks of the financial industry. The technology of blockchain can allow you to save billions of dollars. A current report of Goldman Sachs suggested that it may save almost $6 billion in a year.

Initially, banks were hesitating to explore these unique technologies because of their reasonable concerns regarding potential fraud. They started an investigation into the working procedures of blockchain and its cost savings by allowing the back-office settlement mechanism to practice trades, transactions and transfers at a faster rate.

The initial international transactions of blockchain were concluded on 24th October 2016. It was brokered by the WFC (Wells Fargo & Co) and Commonwealth Bank of Australia, the deal of $35,000 involve cotton trader of Australia Brighann Cotton Marketing that purchased 88 cotton bales from its Texas division in the U.S. and sent it to China, Qingdao.

Tech Companies and Blockchains

To attract the middleman and move toward decentralization and democratization, tech startups are espousing blockchain technology to disrupt a number of industries. Among business startups leveraging blockchain technology for the Internet of Things devices in 21 Inc., the startup based on Silicon Valley receive $116 million funding in 2015. As per this firm, the funding will be utilized to embed mining chips of Bitcoin into associated cell phones and IOT devices.

A P2P lending platform known as BTC Jam headquartered in San Francisco, specializes in offering Bitcoin-based debts. Over the preceding year, the organization has lent $15 million or even more. Storj is the only company currently doing beta-testing for the development of cloud-based storage on the blockchain-powered network. They want to improve the security while reducing the dependency of users on the centralized system of single storage. The organization offers the opportunity to users to rent out additional storage capacity, similar to property owners who rent out additional rooms.

Proof of Existence is a financial company to utilize blockchains for implementing contracts. It utilizes DLT to store encoded information and enable a transaction that can't be replicated to be interrelated to a document.

Established firms like MSFT (Microsoft Corporation) are also interested in blockchain technology. They have recently formed a partnership with ConsenSys blockchain firm. In the month of December 2015, ConsenSys and Microsoft announced EBaaS (Ethereum Blockchain) service on Azure. This cloud computing platform of Microsoft offers a cloud-based and single-click environment to developers and clients. It was June 2016, both companies started the development of blockchain-based and open source identity system for services, apps, products, and people.

Benefits of Blockchains

Competences ensuing from DLT may increase some cost savings. DLT systems ensure it for banks and businesses to streamline internal operations, mistakes, delays and dramatically decrease expenses caused by conventional methods for settlement of records.

The widespread approval of DLT can bring huge cost saving in 3 major areas, such as:

- Decrease the processing delay that may decrease capital held against the risk of numerous pending transactions.
- Fully mechanized DLT systems will result in fewer errors and decrease repetitive steps for confirmation.
- It is cheap to maintain electronic ledgers as compared to the traditional accounting system. It can decrease the headcount of employees in offices.

Moreover, you can save money by shrinking the amount of capital required by dealers/brokers to put up to outstanding and unsettled trades. Ease of auditing and transparency must lead to savings in regulatory of anti-money laundering compliance costs. Removal of human involvement in blockchain in processing is beneficial in different cross-border trades. These may take longer because of numerous time-zone issues and all parties should confirm the payment procedure. This system set up payment triggered and smart contracts after meeting particular conditions. The cotton transaction of blockchain uses smart contracts to automatically made half payments as the shipment reached particular geographic milestones.

Chapter 2 – An Overview and Uses of Blockchain

The blockchain technology permanently records the transactions so that no one can erase them, but you can update them. It will help you to keep a nonstop historic trail. Blockchain can't be explained as a phenomenon, but this marching phenomenon is slowly advancing like a tsunami and all-encompassing everything beside its way via its progression. Simply, it is an important overlay over internet. It is often known as a trust layer and the blockchains are mammoth reagents for modification that hit at the governance, customary business models, and ways of life, global intuitions and society.

Blockchain dissemination will be encountered with confrontation because it a risky change. This technology can rebel old concepts that are locked in your mind for various decades. Blockchains can challenge ascendency and mainly controlled methods of carrying out transactions. For instance, there is no need to pay escrows against title insurance because the Blockchain may mechanically evaluate it irrefutably. Blockchains may loosen up trust factor that are in the control of essential organizations, such as makers, banks, policy, clearing houses, large corporations, governments, etc.

This latest technology enables you to dodge the early control points, such as, counterparty validation is easy on blockchain rather than a clearinghouse. Blockchains free the reliance function from outer boundaries similarly as medieval institutions did to relinquish the printing control. It is illusory to limit the blockchain as only a dispersed/distributed ledger. Actually, distributed ledger is an important dimension of blockchain. It is described as a technology or a broadcasting platform. Proponents of blockchain believe that everyone should have access to trust instead of giving it in the hands of dominant forces that control or tax it in the form of free, permissions and access rights.

Trust should be an essential portion of P2P associations and it is often facilitated by technology. Trust is often swapped by cryptographic evidences and maintained via a trusted computer network to confirm its security. This technology is taken as an innovative method for the implementation of reliable transactions without reliable mediators. Transitional controlled trust arose with minor friction, but the trust of blockchain is free from friction. It follows a particular path with limited struggle and gradually become decentralized toward the boundaries of the particular network. Blockchain enables properties and worth to be swapped and provide a speedy rail to move the all kinds of values without any intermediaries.

In the perspective of back-end substructure, the blockchains are allegorically the eventual and non-stop workstations. Once they launched, they will not go down, but offer an implausible resiliency. Nothing to worry about failure unlike bank system and cloud services because these services can easily go down. The internet had replaced some intermediaries, but now blockchain is also swapping other mediators. It is about creating a new one and it is essential for current intermediaries to find out their roles and effects of these roles, while every other may angle for the piece of a new pie to decentralize the process.

In short, the blockchain technology is an essential need of the current era and this book is designed to share valuable details of Bitcoin. You will read about practical uses of blockchain and its effectiveness in the financial market.

"In financial markets, there's always a mechanism to correct an attack. In a blockchain, there is no mechanism to correct it — people have to accept it."- Robert Sams, founder and chief executive of London-based Clearmatics.

Once an existing block completes, a new block will be generated. These blocks are closely linked to each other similar to a chain in a proper linear and chronological order. Each new block contains a dash of the previous block. In order to use traditional banking as an analogy, the blockchain has a history of previous banking transactions. You can find bitcoin transactions in a chronological order, similar to bank transactions. Blocks can be taken as individual financial statements. Blockchain has a complete record of every transaction of bitcoin. It provides insight, facts, the value of patents and other essential points.

Some developers believe in starting looking at the creation of various blockchains because they don't want to depend on a solitary blockchain. Sidechains and parallel blockchains will be helpful for tradeoffs and enhance the scalability with the use of independent and alternative blockchains. It will increase the chances of innovation.

Example of Blockchain

To understand the blockchain concept, there is an example of a product known as Gyft. It is an online platform to sell gift cards where the customers can redeem, buy and sell gift cards. This business is a partnership between a 44-year old merchant or FinTechn organization First Data and the infrastructure of blockchain provides Chain to provide gift cards of SMBs with the help of blockchains. This product will be rolled out and become a solid example of blockchain-based modernism that has no connection with bitcoin. It is considered as a part of blockchain because a majority of SMBs doesn't have any gift card program and POS that are installed at SMBs may not accept them.

It is really expensive to offer a program for the gift card and hard to notice the immediate benefits. It can postpone fulfillment for a retailer, but large retailers can understand it in a better way or accept gift cards. Blockchain enables Gyft to offer a gift card solution for the customers of SMB.

Advantages of Blockchain Technology

- Blockchain can work as a public ledger system to record and authenticate all transactions to make them reliable and secure.
- All transactions are authentic by miners that make these transactions immutable and avoid any hacking threat.
- In the presence of blockchain technology, there is no need to involve any third party or middle authority for successful peer-to-peer transactions.

Devolution of the Technology

Financial institutions and banks are investing their time and money and there are some banks that have shown an intention on the blockchain. There are a few reports that the derivatives groups, clearing houses and Deutsche Boerse along with EuroCCP are working on the uses of blockchain in clearing areas. The Western union may also look into Ripple technology to learn more about blockchain. Some banks experiment with the blockchain technology and there are a few examples:

Fidor Bank

This bank is working in a partnership to provide EU and bitcoins as an exchange of digital currency. They exchange with P2P BTC and Bitcoin.de trading platforms in Germany. They started a partnership with Ripple labs to offer money transfer services.

LHV Bank

They have started working on the blockchain project in the middle of 2014. They designed an app based on Cuber Wallet in the middle of 2015. They are working in a partnership with coin floor and coin base and experimenting digital security along with blockchain.

CBW Bank, Cross River Bank:

They are a partner with Ripple labs to design risk management structure and offer cheap remittance services.

Goldman Sachs

They participated as a lead investor in the $50 million funding round of startup Circle-Internet-Financial Ltd. They extensively prepare reports on blockchain and bitcoin to publish in their annual publication.

BBVA Ventures

They invest in coin base and share a research report to explain their interest in the latest blockchain technology.

Santander

They claim to have 20 to 25 cases for the blockchain and work with a small team called "Crypto 2.0" to find out the accurate uses of blockchain in banking.

Westpac

Westpac was working in partnership with Ripple to design a cheap and widely used payments platform. The Reinventure called its VC arm, took part in Coinbase's $75M Series-C funding.

Barclays Bank

The bank contains two labs for bitcoin in London and these are open for numerous blockchain and bitcoin entrepreneurs, businesses and coders. They are working in partnership with Safello and develop various banking services for blockchain.

They are running accelerators to offers mentoring to blockchain enthusiasts and a chance to work along with the bank on particular projects. They claim to have almost 45 experiments that they are interested in doing internally.

Chapter 3 – Role of Blockchain in Economy and Financial Services

Bitcoin can be used as a digital currency because you can pay for various goods and services. Every transaction of Bitcoin is recorded in the block or a data file. A new block is created with the help of a computer code after completely filling the old block. You can build a constant strand of records that are commonly known as blockchain. This technology is unique because it can make your work easy. In its presence, there is no need to use a central source, like a traditional bank to confirm the bitcoin exchanges. This certification is provided by "miners". Miners are the creative people who create safe blocks by lending computing powers for the solution of complicated math problems. After cracking each problem, a new block is automatically added to this chain and the miners get Bitcoins for these services.

Every computer code in the time-stamped block is built on the preceding block and it becomes impossible to go back and change your old blocks. Bitcoin always transfers the records to this blockchain database and the startup is used as a proof of subsistence. Every time, it requires blockchain to record a cryptographic assimilate of the document and validate the users own these files at this particular time. It is useful to verify patents and copyrights of particular materials. Onename is a startup to offer an ID for blockchain and a digital passport for the identification of users. To identify verifications, you can start voting via smartphones.

Deloitte Canada is a professional service and it will lead the investigation team to focus on the work of blockchain and similar technologies. These technologies are often used to make audits precise. The amount of financial information and a large number of transactions can make the work of an auditor difficult, but the auditors can select a sample from the set of numerous transactions. They will try to verify the authentication of the audit of a particular company and its balance. With the use of blockchain, it is easy to confirm a wide range of financial transactions to confirm an exchange. This exchange is often recorded in the blockchain.

Blockchain technology is a unique innovation since the advent of the internet. This industry is started looking to influence it to transfer and store its value to other monetary instruments. Capital market is an important industry in the financial space where the experts are optimistic about the use of this technology

This technology has the potential to transfigure financial transactions, but there are a few challenges and the company should overcome these challenges in order to experience lots of benefits. This technology was developed along with the digital cryptocurrency bitcoin. This special currency act like a decentralized ledger to record each transaction and store the essential details on the worldwide network to avoid tampering. Bitcoin is a virtual currency that enables users to swap online credit for essential goods and services. Different organizations looked into alternative apps for the advanced blockchain, other than any digital currency.

For example. Nasdaq allows investors to securely vote at the meeting of shareholders with its trialing system. Bank of America has several blockchain related patents.

Bitcoin is a technology behind the bitcoin that is unfortunate which creates relations with drug site (Silk Road) or the contortions of the Bitcoin. It clears that the Blockchain reflects a unique technology with an ability to change the life cycle of the transaction of the securities. Blockchain enables value to store in a secure environment on an individual level. You can transfer the value of a chain to broker and investor.

It is essential to overcome the legal and regulatory hurdles. Try to tackle the political roadblocks and finally fit the blockchain technology in the market environment that is far better than proof of value and exchange. Regulators typically focus on the safety of assets and projection of the rights of investors and finality of settlement. These all can be safeguarded during the age of blockchain. There are a few challenges in the adoption of blockchain technology:

Top Standards of Technology

You have to set high standards for security, performance, and robustness of blockchain. You will need integration with the existing non-blockchain systems, such as you will need a risk management platform.

Upgrading of Legislations and Regulations

Latest regulatory principles should be integrated to make blockchain technologies as an important part of the infrastructure of the market.

Governance and Standards

At particular design points, you will need industry alignments, such as permission-based access or open system. The principle of appropriateness (in interaction with the financial ledgers and the interoperability between the networks) may run different protocols and offer protection against errors of coding.

Transition Risk

You should reduce the operational risk and this move will need a quick recovery of participants to relapse to the customary ecosystem as a contingency.

Chapter 4 – Relation of Coinbank and Cryptocurrencies

CoinBanks gets lots of hype in the internet world because of its status and other fraudulent companies. People often share their concerns about this platform because there are numerous spams and frauds over the internet. I am going to share unknown facts with all of you about CoinBanks.

CoinBanks is an online investment planning service that proves helpful for investors to enjoy the benefits of cryptocurrencies. CoinBanks allow you to invest in the portfolios of cryptocurrencies designed to spread risk while you are taking benefits of the precariousness of cryptocurrencies. CoinBanks has been working since 1999 and it is a primary trading platform for cryptocurrencies and managed to build a good reputation in the market. Just because of their good reputation, the CoinBank has a solid clientele. They ensure the safety of Bitcoin and money of clients with the use of tested methods and effective strategies to grow funds for investors.

CoinBanks developed a new strategy in 2005 and generate high return within 60 days. They collected massive data from major conversation rates in the world by trading volume and load it on the multifunctional model. The strategy became really profitable. After three years, the PAMM account was launched for traders to closely work with PAMM account manager to make a huge profit without investing excessive money.

PAMM Accounts

CoinBank offers 6 types of special PAMM accounts for its clients, such as VIP, Diamond, Platinum, Gold, Silver, and Bronze. These accounts were designed to increase the investment capital for the management of Forex traders.

Investors can securely invest in PAMM account to secure maximum profit with less involvement. You should carefully select a broker and manager for PAMM account after evaluating the potential for profit and risk. Here is a brief overview of the accounts of CoinBanks:

- **VIP:** If you have $250,000, you can sign up for VIP account and get leverage X7 along with all services of platinum account.
- **Diamond:** For a diamond account, you will need $100,000 to sign up. It offers all services of a platinum account and X5 leverage.
- **Platinum:** This special account offers an X3 leverage with the services of chief account analyst, regular signal services and education package with $50,000 amount for registration.
- **Gold:** You will need $10,000 to sign up for this account. You may receive three signals on

a weekly basis and three education sessions along with all services of silver account.

- **Silver:** It offers X2 leverage just like Bronze account. Moreover, the traders can get additional services like personal account analyst, three signals in a week and 2 education sessions after paying $5,000.
- **Bronze:** If you want to sign up for a Bronze account, you will need $2,000 and manager for personal account along with one signal in a week.

Along with Bitcoins, you will find numerous other digital and cryptocurrencies. These are used to invest funds in the CoinBanks. It enables you to trade in multiple currencies instead of putting your all eggs in the same basket. After investing in cryptocurrency, there is nothing to worry about because it will make your life quite simple. If you are interested in a trade, just open the menu of cryptocurrencies and choose your desired currency. You can trade in each currency without opening an account. If you have more than one accounts, it will automatically dilute the ability to trade. It requires funds for trading in different currencies.

Just like other currencies, Bitcoins are simple to trade. It is similar to other currencies in function, but it is different in terms of unpredictability and volatility. To become successful in Bitcoin trading, you should have a successful strategy to follow. It will increase your success chances and decrease your risk. Keep an eye on the position of Bitcoin and rethink about its position with the passage of time.

The price of currencies may go up and down; therefore, you should consistently keep an eye on the trading news. It is difficult to react immediately as you get a news because the market is really volatile. The price may rise or fall to a particular percentage. Just read the news and find the time when you can earn a profit.

Fundamental analysis is essential to get familiar to investors of the stock market and make a successful strategy for Bitcoin trading. Just analyze the fundamental data that affects the number of wallets, per day transactions, active wallets and price. You should learn about overvalued and undervalued bitcoins and make selling and buying decisions accordingly. There are numerous indicators and tools to reduce risk and increase profit. Learn about limit orders and stop your losses. It will increase your profitability and decrease the chances of profit.

You can follow different investment strategies, such as day-trading, riding the trend, short selling and leveraging and swing trading. You can visit their website to learn about these strategies. Bitcoin is infancy and helps you to earn a profit with a small investment. Before investing your money, carefully evaluate the type of currency, its volatility, and other features. Choose an investment strategy as per the nature of currency to increase the rate of return and decrease chances of risk.

Education

A separation section in CoinBank is education that offers detailed information about Bitcoin trading. Moreover, you can find details of different tools that prove helpful for you to take your trading decisions along with different approved models for trading.

News and Exchange

This news section is separate on a site that offers updated information about the market. It proves useful to enable investors and traders to make wise and quick decisions. Furthermore, CoinBanks has some recommendations about exchanges on the websites that currently include BTCC, KRAKEN, BitStamp, and CoinBase.

Chapter 5 – Understand the Future of the Blockchain and its Impact on Industries

Do you know digital currency is not just a currency, but it is more than that? It refers to a new financial model. The people are not sure about the effectiveness of the new model. It is significant to understand the structure of the Bitcoin. It serves as a digital medium to carry out monetary transactions. It reduces the need for paper currency and coins to make various payments. The digital currency is almost 6 years old and its critics have almost declared it as dead. It will be quite interesting to know the Bitcoins future. The experts are expecting that it is going to dislodge the dollar. It is a powerful innovation in the financial world in the previous 500 years.

Working of Bitcoin and Other Digital Currencies

The function of Bitcoin and other digital currencies can be quite confusing. Only a dollar or a gold coin is taken into account as currency and mode of payment. Now imagine that a Bitcoin is a digital currency equal to a dollar bill. The Bitcoins survive as the blockchain in the public ledger and accounting system. You can use a secret password to transfer money to someone else's account.

Future of Bitcoin as Digital Currency

The Bitcoin utilizes in every digital and international transaction. It categorizes as a digital currency. It may involve temporary credit, security against phony withdrawals and fees. You need to pay taxes and particular charges for the delay payments also. The payment transactions with Bitcoin can be simple and secure. It is free of extra charges and time.

Immediate Settlement with Bitcoin

It is possible adjust the Bitcoin immediately similar to cash. There is no need to worry about a number of credit card and security details. You can process every transaction without giving your personal details. The Bitcoin Futures Market enables you to complete a transaction without paying an extra fee.

Better in Stability Than Conventional Currencies

The Bitcoin is an independent and stable currency as compared to any traditional currencies. It is different than euros and dollars. The value of Bitcoin may fluctuate on a frequent basis. The current value equals about $140 in the United States. In the previous year, the value reached up to $12, but it was a temporary effect. The current value of Bitcoin is quite higher than before.

Exchange Value Matters

Exchange value is important for the people looking to invest in the Bitcoin. The Bitcoin users want it for regular transactions for daily possessions and services. The Bitcoin will make arithmetical expenditures promising for the people without a PayPal account. It may reduce the complications involved in the credit system. It requires in various areas of Africa, South Asia, and Latin America. In these regions, the folks have no entree to the digital payments. The Bitcoin infrastructure is almost free for everyone.

No Transaction Fee

The BitPay may convert the Bitcoins into numerous native currencies without any transaction fee. The electronic equipment, hosting companies and international business organizations will play an important role. These may play an important role in the market.

If you know more reasons that we miss in this article, don't forget to share them with us. We will make sure to include these reasons in the next post. Keep it in mind that your feedback is quite valuable to us. It will help us to improve our work in compliance with your needs.

Top Reasons Investors can Save Bitcoin by fighting its volatility

Bitcoin always remains in the headlines because of a constant fluctuation in the value of the currency. There are a permanent rise and fall in the value of the currency. You can get updated details about the price and security risks on government websites. The investor should read this information before investing your money. There are various factors responsible for the increase or decrease in the value of the currency. The interruption of the government in the trade is the biggest reason for this fluctuation.

Reduce the Liabilities Associated with Bitcoins

Dramatic fluctuation in the Bitcoin value can increase or decrease your liabilities. The situation is dangerous for the investor because he may lose his money. The recent law of China is the recent example of the fluctuation in the value of Bitcoin. In the last year, there was a restriction on the trade of Bitcoin in China. It became the reason for the fall in the value of the currency. Keep an eye on the Bitcoin price to analyze the risks involved in the trade with Bitcoin. If you want to decrease the liability and risk associated with the Bitcoin, it will be good to convert the currency at the end of each business day.

The Elliptic vault offers an insurance for your security. This service will provide security and confidence to the business organizations trading with Bitcoin. There are some restrictions for particular industries on the use of Bitcoin. These industries are financial service providers, telecommunication, and research industries. These restrictions can help you to reduce the liability linked to the cryptographic currency.

Improve the Chances of its Adoption as a Virtual Currency

Bitcoin is expected to have a bright future in the emerging markets. There are some steps that can control the stock volatility of the Bitcoin:

The Bitcoin Needs to be Less Volatile

An increase in the volatility can kill the demands of the Bitcoin currency. It is important to reduce the volatility as the customers start using it as a currency. Some apps like BitPay are used to reduce the volatility and increase the adoption. It can help consumers connect with lots of merchants who accept the currency.

More Exchange Platforms are Required

The Bitcoin requires an exchange platform to buffer it from the failures. A trusted network is required. The Bitcoin wallet has an important role in controlling the liquidity of the Bitcoin. Liquidity is required to increase or decrease the volatility. There is a need to have a trusted exchange to deal with currency. Bitcoin needs to be used as an alternative currency of the country.

It Needs to be traded for Cash

In the Arab market, the people don't rely on the online credit cards. The credit penetration rates may vary based on the online transactions. The users need instant money transfer, and the use of Bitcoin as cash will increase its value. The Coinapult will be helpful to transfer Bitcoin on SMS. It will increase the value of Bitcoin currency and decrease the risks associated with it.

Chapter 6 – How does blockchain work and secure data?

The blockchain is an unassailable public record of important data secured via a network system of peer-to-peer participants. You can modify an entry, but unable to remove it. Bitcoin is the main currency application for this unique platform. There are five ideas to use blockchain in the work in progress phase:

Deal out Cloud Storage

Blockchain proposes a method to securely store data of a P2P network in contradiction of cloud storage services, such as Google Drive, Amazon, and Dropbox. You can rely on a solo party instead of relying on various platforms. It works similar to torrents and you can store data at an agreed cost (pre-agreed). Hash data at multiple locations to secure it for a longer period of time. Fathom and Storj.io are two start-ups to explore this idea. After the encryption of data, it is sent out to a network with basic metadata.

Asset Ledger

This absolute public ledge enables you to track the ownership of the world assets via involved bits of data. You have to use private keys adjusted by the owners to access this data. The receptacles of private keys are entitled to exchange assets and view the transmissions on a clear ledger at the real time. Regulator of a digitized asset may lie with private key owner. This key can be transferred with the title to an asset. These keys are used to access a car, house, financial asset, virtualized asset and land titles. This will expressively reduce the cost to make the procedure of asset movement easy as compared to federal resolutions.

Regionalized Notary

Timestamp feature is an exciting feature of blockchain and the entire network typically validate the wrapped pieces of any data known as a hash during a particular period. As a decentralized trustless network, it is important to corroborate the actuality of anything at a particular time that future provable in the law court. Right now, merely integrated solicitor services may particularly dole out this purpose. For instance, you have a particular portion of work. If you want to get started your work, you can get it in arithmetical form and compress it on one hash and transmit it as one transaction. It may enter one block and timestamps efficiently to confirm that you may have initially.

Smart Contracts

These are officially binding digitized agreements recorded on blockchain. They are really smart because they are self-executed and automated. Developers employ the authorized contracts as statements and variables that can be used to released funds with the help of Bitcoin system as a third party facilitator instead of believing a solo authority. For instance, if two people are interested in exchanging $100 at a particular time in the future, a set of preconditions will meet and the details of parties and payout may be programmed into any smart contract. After meeting the defined conditions, funds can be released and sent to the suitable party as per terms.

Decentralized Exchanges

Conventionally, you will require exchanges as an arbitrator, such as clearinghouse or broker to counterpart sellers and buyers. With the help of blockchain, you need to be scraped for the third-party arbiter. In order to sell or buy, you can match and execute with the use of escrow system and the network become a validator. Counterparty runs a decentralized that let the users create their own assets that can be easily exchanged. It helps the users to create their own digital assets that will be exchanged. On the marketplace, orders will be public and matching bids and ask to execute without an intermediary.

The system of malt and escrow signature features combined to release assets and funds when the seller and buyer make an agreement. Most of the applications are under development under Bitcoin 2.0 projects. Future potential of advanced blockchain technology is unraveling, but this application is becoming mainstream.

Other Uses of Blockchain Technology

There is a list of all possible uses of Blockchain that can help you to understand the scope of this unique technology:

It is used to record financial instruments and models, such as:

It is used to record financial instruments and models, such as:
- Private equities
- Currency

- Public equities
- Bonds
- Derivatives
- Voting rights (linked to any one of the above)
- Spending records
- Commodities
- Trading records
- Loan records/ Mortgage
- Crowd-funding
- Servicing records
- Micro-charity
- Micro-finance

You can use it for the various kinds of public records, such as:

- Vehicle registries
- Vehicle registries
- Business license
- Land titles
- Passports
- Regulatory records

- Dissolution records/ Business incorporation
- Records of business ownership
- Criminal records
- Death certificates
- Birth certificates
- Health and Safety Inspections
- Voting
- Voter IDs
- Building permits
- Forensic evidence
- Gun permits
- Court records
- Non-profit records
- Voting records
- Transparency/ non-profit accounting/ Government
- III. Private Records
- Signatures
- Contracts
- Trusts
- Escrows
- Wills

- GPS trails (personal)

IV. Semi-Public Records
- Certifications
- Degree
- Grades
- HR records (performance reviews, salary, accomplishment)
- Medical records
- Learning Outcomes
- Accounting records
- Records of Business transaction
- GPS trails
- Arbitration
- Delivery records

V. Keys of Physical Asset
- Timeshare keys and Vacation home
- Home and apartment keys
- Keys of Hotel Room
- Car keys (personal, rental and leased cars)
- Keys of Safety deposit box
- Locker keys

- Records of Fantasy sports
- Betting records
- Package delivery (key is divided between the receiver and delivery firm)

VI. Intangibles
- Vouchers
- Coupons
- Movie tickets
- Reservations (queues, restaurants, hotels, etc.)
- Patents
- Trademarks
- Copyrights
- Software licenses
- Licenses of video game
- Domain names
- Book/video/music licenses (DRM)
- Online identities
- Authorship proof / Prior art proof

VI. Other

- Documentary records (audio, video, photo)
- Data records (temperature, sports scores, etc.)
- Identity of GPS network
- SIM Cards
- Spam control (micro-payments is required for posting)
- Codes to unlock the gun
- Codes of Weapons unlock codes
- Codes to launch nuclear weapons

Chapter 7 – Industries that Blockchain will Disrupt in the Future

Blockchain serves as a backbone for bitcoin and in 2015, there was a huge bang of this technology in finance. It is obvious that a new technology requires lots of groundwork, such as libraries and a deep database. In 2016, you can notice the emergence of strong technical individuals and it provides a strong base for the infrastructure of the blockchain. Various companies talk about the use of the blockchain network to trade, manage and issue assets, such as financial securities. There is a huge discussion about the little implementation of this useful technology. Most interesting and prominent application is developed by Overstock for the company having SEC approval to issue stock with this technology.

Work of Overstock will be a leading path for the widespread use of Blockchain. This unique technology behind the Bitcoin has the capacity to change money and business matters in the world. Bitcoin is taken as a prominent proof that the blockchain technology can work. This technology is an advanced database that leads people to transfer goods and particular information about value. Blockchain technologies can dominate the future of finance. A perceptible currency with a proficient infrastructure can reduce the cost for all participants of the market. It can change the method of global banking. Bitcoin can make the payments as easy as the communication became easy after the arrival of email.

Potential Changes

The Central bank will adopt blockchain and currencies with cryptographic security will be widely used.

Nasdaq may introduce blockchain-enabled ledger digital technology. This technology will be used to enhance and expand the capabilities of equity management.

Settlement of currency, fixed income, and equity trades are immediate through distributed ledgers and create important opportunities for banks to increase efficiency and create classes of new assets.

Proper Control

- Blockchain and other similar technologies have great potential to reduce the cyber risks via identity authentication and visible ledger.
- Requirements for numbering, indexing, and maintenance records are easy with the help of a special electronic ledger system.
- Car rental agencies will be able to get the advantage of smart contracts and enable rentals to receive payment and confirm

the essential information through the records of the blockchain.

- Some refrigerators are designed with sensors and have the ability to connect to the internet. These types of refrigerators can automatically interact with the external world and manage automated interactions. They can order food for you and make payment. These are designed in a way to automatically upgrade their software.

- Small business organizations trust in the blockchain to create reliable and trusted platforms for trading.

- Blockchain has the ability to bring transparency and robustness to the post-trade environment.

- Blockchain uses new technologies to reduce the chances of cyber risks and offer authentication of through visible ledger.

- It enables banks to pay instantly to your supplier on the internet. It can modify the timing of the risk.

Track Down Crime

- Latest startup of blockchain claims that its software can track down criminals at a faster rate and reduce your expense.
- Connecticut warns parents that latest Darknet cryptocurrencies are known as Bitcoin and these could be blamed for helping juvenile drinkers to get droned.

Implication of Bitcoin Technology

Blockchain technology has the potential to replace central banks. It can promote the use of cryptographically protected currencies. This technology can reduce the cost of USB infrastructure in trade of securities, regulatory compliance, and cross-border payments.

Blockchain technology has the potential to disrupt current technologies and create various new industrial opportunities. It can make the world smaller by increasing the efficiency and speed of transactions.

Cryptocurrencies and bitcoin can be used for the distribution of social welfare in the developing nations. The procedure of election is really grueling and expensive, but with the help of blockchain technology, these will be easy and cheap.

While discussing the value of the digital currency, the Bitcoin Gold Standard can't be ignored because it is more precious than any metal. The Bitcoin hopes to get more users to increase its viability in the mainstream market. A software program is being used all around the world to follow a mathematical method for the production of bitcoins. This formula is available for everyone.

Chapter 8 – Cryptocurrency, Blockchain and Bitcoin

Cryptocurrency aka digital currency is based on cryptography for optimum security; therefore, it is really difficult to counterfeit it. For the secure transfer of currency from one person to another, different public and private keys are often used. The first cryptocurrencies were Bitcoin traded in 2009 and now, numerous cryptocurrencies are available in the market. Different ethics of cryptography are used for circulation, decentralization, and security of important economic information. The notable difference between cryptocurrencies and fiat money is fewer chances of acceleration, spectacular act and other ways of money abuse in the creation of money. Cryptocurrency is a defined process bounded with publically and privately known value.

Specifications of Cryptocurrencies

Lots of cryptocurrencies are available and the specifications of all other currencies are quite similar to Bitcoin. Cryptocurrency system supports safety, veracity, and equilibrium of all journals from a group of mutually skeptical parties. Some miners and active associates of the community maintain the security of the system by increasing the difficulty level of the whole system. It is mathematically possible to ward off the fundamental sanctuary of a cryptocurrency, but its price may be ridiculously elevated. Take the example of Bitcoin's POW (proof-of-work) based structure that is easy to attack through mathematics. An attacker needs great computation power to control the entire horde of miners with $1 / 2^{\wedge}(\#$ validation circles for the cryptocurrency $- 1)$. It is really a difficult task to evade the security of Bitcoin proof-of-work.

Circulation of Cryptocurrencies

In January 2014, fiat money is replaced with cryptocurrency by no nation. Cryptocurrencies proved helpful to introduce new units of currency and to place a decisive cap on the total amount of legal tender that will even be in the stream. This is important to imitate the paucity and the worth of valuable material, and to dodge the situation of hyperinflation. This may raise the situation of hyperdeflation because the growing popularity of money and amount of currency circulating in the market may approach the finite cap.

Ordinary currencies are usually kept by monetary institutions because the susceptibility of cryptocurrencies are low to convulsion by law administration. Current cryptocurrencies all are pseudonymous, though accompaniments like Zerocoin and disseminated laundry features have been recommended, which may permit for obscurity.

Notable Cryptocurrencies

Bitcoin 2009 with code BTC, Ripple 2013 with code XPR, Litecoin 2011 with code LTC, Peercoin 2012 with code PPC, Namecoin 2011 with code

NMC and Dogecoin 2013 with code DOGE are some notable cryptocurrencies.

How should Bitcoin be seen as more mainstream?

It is really astonishing that the interest on the Bitcoin is rising exponentially with the increase in the value of the currency. In this situation, there is a common question in the mind of every one, "Can Bitcoin become a major stream currency one day beside the dollar, Euro, Pound and other national currencies."

Future of the Bitcoin

In the recent months, the Bitcoin is grabbing maximum media attention, and as a result, the people are taking more interest in the digital currency and increasing the use as well as investment in Bitcoin. This shows that there are lots of potential benefits of the expansion of the Bitcoin market. There are a sudden rise and fall in the value, and according to the situation, it can be said that the infrastructure of the Bitcoin is unacceptable. The trading exchanges for Bitcoin are proletarian to some extent, because due to DDoS attacks, support issues, security problems and poor interfaces, there are serious threats to the mainstream Forex trading systems. It is really hard to get statistical data and index chart from these exchanges. Even in the presence of all these reasons, the Bitcoin is continuously grabbing the attention of people, and the currency is becoming popular day by day.

It is still not obvious about the future of Bitcoin on the side of public banks because this currency is a major threat to their position in the market. Ironically, some people feel that the currency should be frozen out, instead of ignoring it, because, in the non-financial sector, it may open new ideas for better services. There are some rumors that some high profile companies are showing their interest in the Bitcoin, and these companies are ready to invest in the infrastructure of the currency to propel the sector in the upward direction in a more professional manner. There is a possibility about the entry of giant Forex trading institutions in the Bitcoin. The biggest problem with the Bitcoin is its tendency to rise fast in the value, and the deliberate upper limit can be the reason behind it.

Deflationary Nature of the Bitcoin

The Bitcoins intrinsic the deflationary nature, and this will be the biggest disadvantage for the economy. With the growth of the economy, it is important to slowly and steadily increase the supply of currency. Absolute ceiling on the highest number of coins is not good for the growing economy. The huge difference between the other currencies and Bitcoin will make it a bad option for the economy. The economy should possess the ability to expand the money supply, according to the demand. In 2008 and 2009, there was a global banking crisis and to solve this problem, the concerned department focused on the economy to save it from the crises, because any crash can increase the unemployment and drastic increase in the money supply. With Bitcoin, it is really hard for you to manage all this.

Sound money has its own importance, but the people like to save maximum money instead of spending it. The Bitcoin has an intrinsic tendency to deflate. To increase the value of Bitcoin, the standalone transaction serves as a medium for different purchases.

Heavy Price Fluctuations of the Bitcoin

The Bitcoin is highly volatile; therefore it is not taken as a reliable form of money to transfer because of its fluctuation value. Bitcoin still has some major advantages for zero cost of the transaction and high speed. The volatile nature of the coin means it is perfect to use for purchases after converting it in the real-time currency check at the point of purchase. It is difficult to price goods in the Bitcoin because it is important to know the cost in Euro and Dollar in advance, but it is not easy.

People feel hesitant to make the transaction with the currency having fluctuating values during the course of 24 hours. A currency that can't be the real currency that is difficult to use confidently and safely for various transactions. The currency can be used as the reference of euro and dollar while making payments with the Bitcoin.

A peer to peer transfer system is the biggest positive point of the Bitcoin because the transfer is absolutely free and no need to deal with bank bureaucracy to pay different fees and charges. As per the constituted rights, the Bitcoin can be used as a long-term store of value just like gold and any other precious item. For the long-term purpose, it is fine, but in the short run, it can be risky to use Bitcoin as digital gold.

Conflicts of Bitcoin with Monetary Policy of the Government

Governments always find the ways to control the value of the currency in their territory in order to finance the debts of the public. Bitcoin can be the problem for the government to manage the spending of government and taxes. There will be a great deal of the loss by combining independent currency with Bitcoin, because it may try to take over the currency in the mainstream of the economy. They may lose control over currency, and there will be the same situation caused by Euro in the southern European countries. This is the main reason for central banks and governments to not submissively accept Bitcoin going mainstream without a sound reason.

Possible Options for Bitcoin in the Future

- Although the government and banks are not accepting Bitcoin, in future, the Bitcoin may take off and become widely used currency. Its general acceptance level can bring it in the line with national currencies and the Euro.

- It may also happen that the Bitcoin rise heavily in value and then crash at the same level for the horrible loss for most of the people.

- It can also be possible that a better digital currency can diminish the value of Bitcoin because currently there are lots of other digital currencies in the phase of development.

- The government may acknowledge the Bitcoin idea and make all other national currencies digital. They may switch all currencies from peer to peer system, or any other similar system.

Chapter 9 – Challenges for Blockchain Technology

Blockchain technology is one of the most troublesome innovations since the advent of the internet. This industry is started looking to influence it to transfer and store its value to other monetary instruments. The capital market is an important industry in the financial space where the experts are optimistic about the use of this technology.

Technical Analysis for Trading in Digital Currencies

The technical analysis, also known as security analysis is used to forecast the direction of the prices and volume. The analysis can help you to know about the stock market prices in different states. Charts are a commonly used method for the Stock Market Technical Analysis because it will help you to identify the price patterns and market trends. The analysts prefer to use market indicators of various types to assess the trending of assets and the relationship between price/volume and the market indicators. The technical analysis requires different prototypes and transaction directions based on the strength of the catalogue, moving medians, relapses, intra-market and inter-market price associations, trade cycles and stock market trends.

Following are some reasons that may help you to understand that why Stock Market Technical Analysis is better for the long-term stock trading:

Stock Price Reflection Via Market News

The analysis will help you to know about stock prices and the stock price is a reflection of all the fundamental market news. Psychology of the crowded market can be identified with the use of patterns. It also helps to forecast the price and enables investors to take a right financial decision.

Identification of Crowded Trend

The Stock Market Technical Analysis will help you to know the direction of the stock market trend. There can be different trends in stock, such as it can be an uptrend, a downtrend, or a sideways trend. The information about the direction of the trend proves helpful because when you are investing money in the long term stocks.

Recommendations about the Entry and Exit

While investing in the long-term stocks, it is important to have your entry and exit strategy for long-term trading in the technical analysis. The fundamental analysis is important to determine the long-term entry and exit points. The important news is available for the stock price and change in the market. For Stock Market Technical Analysis, some traders preferably use indicators, volume, pattern and moving average find out the entry and exit points.

Technical Indicators and Triggers

Technical indicators and triggers prove helpful to figure the historical price and the volume of purchases. The selling movement of the stock is also important to track that helps you to obtain the average price movement of your stock in the present and potential movement in the future.

Future Price Movement

The Technical Analysis of technical data will help you to check the future price movements with the use of technical formula. It will predict the share price and its movements in the future. The potential time and extensions in the trends will be a good indicator of the price movement.

These all points will help you to know the value and the fluctuation rate of the long-term stock. The Stock Market Technical Analysis will help you to find out the market trends, current price and the movements of the currency prices.

Chapter 10 – Basic Terminology of Blockchain and Financial Market

Particular terminology is used to explain different aspects of the blockchain. See the basic terminology of the blockchain.

Address

Cryptocurrency address is used to send and receive transaction on the network. It is a cord of alphanumeric typescripts to be represented as a QR code (scannable).

Agreement Ledger

It is a distributed ledger used by 2 or even more parties to reach and negotiate an agreement.

Attestation Ledger

It is a durable record of statements, commitments, and agreements to provide attestation (providing evidence) that these statements, commitments and agreements were made.

ASIC

Application Specific Integrated Circuit (ASIC) are silicon chips designed for a single task. For bitcoin, these chips are designed to process SHA-256 hashing problems for the mining of new bitcoins.

Uppercase Bitcoin

These are cryptocurrencies based on the pow (proof-of-work) blockchain.

Lowercase bitcoin

The particular collection of technologies used by the ledger of bitcoin and a special solution. The currency is one of these technologies and offers incentive to miners at the time of mining.

Blockchain

It is a distributed ledger embraced digitally the recorded, unchangeable data in blocks or packages instead of collating them on a solo sheet of paper. Every block is chained to another block with the use of a cryptographic signature. This proves helpful to use blockchain like a ledger. This ledger can be accessed and shared by anyone with suitable permission.

Block Height

Block height means total blocks connected together in a block chain. For instance, 0 height will be the first block. This block is also known as Genesis block.

Block Reward

This reward is given to successful miners after hashing a transaction block. This reward can be a blend of transaction fees and coins as per policy used in question by cryptocurrency. The present block reward for a Bitcoin network is almost 25 bitcoins for every reward.

Central Ledger

It is a ledger maintained by the central agency.

Confirmation

It means the blockchain transactions are verified by a network. It is possible with the help of mining in the proof-of-work system. After confirming a transaction, it can't be doubled or reversed. The confirmation of transaction makes it possible to perform a dual spend attack.

Consensus Process

This procedure involves a group of peers who will be responsible to maintain a distributed ledger to access the consensus of the content of ledger.

Consensus Point

It is a point defined in time or volume of records or set number to be auxiliary to ad ledger, where peers come across to agree the ledger's state.

Cryptocurrency

It is a form of currency based on mathematics, where techniques of encryption are utilized to regulate the generation of currency units and verify the transfer of funds. Moreover, central bank independently operates cryptocurrencies.

Digital Identity

It is a networked or online identity claimed or adopted in cyberspace by an organization, electronic device or individual.

Distributed Ledger

These are a particular kind of database that spread across numerous sites, institutions, and countries. Records are a pile up in a consistent ledger. Data of distributed ledger may be "unpermissioned" or "permissioned" to control who should view it.

Difficulty

In the proof-of-work mining, the difficulty means how hard it becomes to verify blocks in the blockchain network. The difficulty of mining is adjusted in the bitcoin networks to verify blocks. They often maintain the block verification time for almost 10 minutes.

Double Spend

This term refers to a scenario in Bitcoin network where a person tries to send a transaction of bitcoin to 2 different recipients simultaneously. After confirming a bitcoin transaction, it is almost impossible to dual spend it. The level of confirmation of a transaction can make it difficult to dual spend the bitcoins.

Genesis Block

It is the very 1st block in the block chain.

Halving

Bitcoins possess a finite supply that makes them a rare digital commodity. The total amount of the bitcoins is almost 21 million. The bitcoin numbers generated in each block is decreased to

50% in every 4 years. This is known as halving. The final halving year will be 2140.

Hashrate

These are the number of hashes may be executed by a miner bitcoin in a particular period of time (typically a second).

ICO (Initial Coin Offering)

An ICO (initial coin offering) is a particular event in which the new cryptocurrency sells tokens (advance tokens) from overall coinbase for upfront capital. These are frequently used for new cryptocurrency developers to increase capital.

Ledger

It is a record store (append-only) where the records are unchallengeable and hold general information than financial records.

Litecoin

It is a p2p (peer-to-peer) cryptocurrency based on a proof-of-work Scrypt network. It is also referred to the silver of the bitcoin's gold.

Mining

The procedure to add and verify transactions to a blockchain. The procedure used to solve cryptographic problems with the use of computing hardware also triggers the issue of cryptocurrencies.

Multi-Signature

Multisig (multi-signature) addresses allow numerous parties to require keys more than 1 for the authorization of a transaction. The required number of signatures are agreed for the creation of each address. The multisig addresses have greater resistance to mugging.

Off-Ledger Currency

It means a currency used on-ledger and imprinted off-ledger. This example can be the use of distributed ledger to deal with a nationwide currency.

On-Ledger Currency

A used on-ledger currency and a minted on-ledger currency. Cryptocurrency bitcoin is its biggest example.

P2P

P2P (peer-to-peer) denotes decentralized interactions between almost 2 parties in a highly interrelated network. Participants of P2P directly deal with every interaction through a solo mediation point.

Peer

He/she is an actor to share responsibility for the maintenance of integrity and identity of a ledger.

Participant

He/she is an actor who can access a ledger, add records to the ledger and read records.

Permissioned Ledger

It is a ledger where the participant should have permission to use and access a ledger. Permissioned ledgers often have 1 or even more owners. With the addition of each new record, the integrity of ledger is checked by a restricted consensus procedure. This is done by government departments or banks.it is essential to make the maintenance of a shared record simply that the consensus procedure used by an unpermissioned ledger. The permissioned blockchains offer highly-verifiable sets of data because the consensus procedure creates a particular digital signature that is visible to all parties. A permissioned journal/ledger is faster than an unpermissioned journal/ledger.

Private Currency

It is a currency distributed by a firm or private individual, typically uninsured assets are used for its security.

Private Key

It is a data string that shows your access to the particular wallet of bitcoins. Private keys may be a password, but it should not be revealed to anyone except you. They permit you to spend bitcoins from your particular bitcoin wallet via a cryptographic signature.

Proof-of-Stake

It is a substitute to the proof-of-work (POW) system. It refers to the use of your current stake in any cryptocurrency (the total amount of cryptocurrency you hold) to calculate the amount of currency that you may mine.

Proof-of-Work

It is a system that ties the capability of mining to computational command. Bitcoin should be hashed that is itself a simple computational procedure, but an extra variable is required for the hashing procedure to make it difficult. After successfully hashing a block, the hashing should be taken some computation effort and time.

Consequently, each hashed block is a proof of work.

Replicated Ledger

It is a ledger with one authoritative (master) copy of data and many non-authoritative (slave) copies.

Ripple

A network of payment built on the distributed ledgers can be used to transfer currencies. The network contains gateways and payment nodes operated by experts. Payments require the use of IOUs series and this network is based on trusted relationships.

SHA 256

It is a cryptographic function utilized on the basis of proof of work system of bitcoin.

Scrypt

It is a substitute proof of work structure to SHA-256. It is famous for its friendly designed to GPU and CPU miners while offering an some benefits to ASIC miners.

Smart Contracts

These are special contracts whose terms are documented in the computer language instead of using legal language. Similar contracts may be mechanically executed by a particular computing system like a suitable disseminated ledger system.

Transaction Block

It is an accumulation, of transactions on a bitcoin network collected into a block that may be hashed and become a part of the blockchain.

Tokenless Ledger

This ledger refers to the distributed ledgers that don't need an innate currency for operation.

Transaction Fee

It is a minute fee imposed to a few transactions sent across the network of bitcoin. The charges of the transaction are bestowed to a miner that effectively hashes a block with relevant transaction.

Unpermissioned Ledgers

These ledgers like Bitcoin without a single owner – indeed, they can't be owned. The objective of each unpermissioned ledger allows anyone to subsidize data to a ledger for each person in possession of a ledger to have alike copies. This generates censorship resistance that means no actor can avoid a transaction from being added to a ledger. Contestants maintain the veracity of a ledger by reaching the consensus of its state.

Business Terms

For your convenience, a few business terms are also available so that you can understand the language of the market.

Market Penetration Price

It is an important strategy that is used to get a dramatic increase in the volume of sales and market saturation of a new product. This approach is used to advertise your product at wide level by keeping the price of new product comparatively low. Market penetration price is an assumption based strategy in which price, demands and profit margin of a specific product is based on assumptions only. It is an important technique to grab the attention of customers toward your new products and services. Its correct application will help you to get desired results. You can easily increase your market share and sales volume with market penetration price.

Holding Company

Holding company is a company that holds outstanding stock of other companies. It is also known as the parent company that gets the authority to control the board of directors of another corporation by getting it's enough voting stock. In order to get the authority to control the board of directors, it is important for the holding company to must have 80 percent voting stock of the said organization. It enables holding the company to enjoy tax-free dividends. It reduces the risk of owners; therefore, companies prefer to get the control of different other companies. Sometimes, the company adds word "Holding" with its name to get the identity of the pure holding company.

Fractional Ownership

It is a technique to diminish the risk of ownership of an extremely precious tangible asset by giving its shares to several distinct parties. A tangible asset can be a jumbo, cruiser or a piece of resort real estate. It is the best technique for those who do not want to bear the heavy loss for the possession of a high-value asset. It is an ability in which you can share maintaining the cost of an asset with other people. Fractional possession requires proper management and administrations under specific rules and regulations. Management is responsible to oversee regular operations and each party is liable to access asset according to his/her share.

Free Market

The free market is completely opposite to controlled market because no designated authority is authorized to proscribe the free market. The free market is directly linked with capitalism in contemporary usage. This market operates with little or no government control. It is considered as an idealized form of the market because the buyers and sellers can easily do a transaction without any state intervention in the form of taxes, subsidies, and regulations. Stocks of free markets are widely traded and these types of markets are advocated by socialists. In simple words, it is a market in which free exchanges take place under a voluntary agreement between two parties in the form of goods and services.

Gift Tax

It is a federal tax that is imposed on an individual for gifting any valuable thing to another person.

Receiving party is not liable to pay the full value of the gift, but some persons may have to pay less amount of the full value of the gift. The sender of the gift is responsible to pay gift tax, but the receiver may pay nothing or a percentage of total value of the gift. There are some persons who are completely excluded from gift tax:

- Spouse
- Political Organization
- Medical and Educational Organization
- Low-value gifts

Every state has its own regulations regarding gift tax; therefore, it is better to consult concerned tax authorities, to check either tax regulations applied to your gift.

Glamour Stock

A stock that is characterized by high earning escalation rate and the price of this stock tends to rice at a faster rate in the bull market as compare to average market. It is a popular stock among investors because of its great growth potential and endurance. It is an expensive stock and has high demand in the market. Institutional investors like to invest in this stock because of great profit earnings ratio. It is the best opportunity for those, who want to double their money without any additional efforts. Shares of glamour stocks are available in the market at highest rates because of their increasing demand.

Goodwill

Goodwill is an intangible asset that is found in the balance sheet in a separate category named as an intangible asset. It is other than a physical asset just like buildings, equipment and machines. Goodwill is an important tangible asset that reflects the value of intangible assets including brand name of the business, good relations with customers and employees, patents and proprietary technology. Goodwill can be increased with the acquisition of another business, and an amount is necessary to be paid to the company according to the book value of intangible assets of the targeted firm. Goodwill is a quantifiable prudent value including the reputation of the organization with its clients.

Graveyard Market

Term "graveyard market" is used for an appropriate description of the market trend referred to the period near the ending stages of a protracted bear market. This market is not appropriate for the long-term investors because of sudden closing. New investors are advised to stay liquid by sidelining their money in cash or cash corresponding securities until the development of market conditions. Investors cannot get maximum out of graveyard market therefore usually investors avoid it. Overall market conditions remain slow to improve but its decisive positive outlook may trap new investors. Long-term investors usually avoid investments in graveyard market because of uncertain conditions.

Green Audit

It is a process to assess environmental impact on the processes, projects, and products of an organization. It is an appropriate technique to find out different ways for the reduction in energy consumption. The green audit is performed to check the impacts of a business on the environment. It involves analysis of green thresholds to determine the potential problems and possible solutions for sustainable developments. It an important evaluation through which a business can find ways to increase its efficiency with environment-friendly methods including renewal of power sources to avoid environment pollutions. New sources can be wind, solar and geothermal energy.

Green Taxes

Green taxes also are known as Ecotax "Ecological Taxation" are taxes imposed on environmental pollutants. Taxes on the polluting emanations are considered important economically to reduce the environmental pollination in an appropriate manner. Green taxes are encouraged by the wrong behavior of firm and households to reduce the pollution. Green taxes are indirect taxes that are imposed to encourage ecologically activities. These taxes are frequently collected in Europe to realize the business organizations that they are doing wrong with the environment. Green tax shift proposal is also offered to reduce the burden of other taxes like human labor and renewable resources.

Gross Domestic Product

It is a fiscal value of all finished goods and services that are manufactured within a country during a specific period of time. GDP is calculated on annual basis by including all public and private consumptions, government expenditures, investments, and exports as well as imports in a defined region.

GDP = C + G + I + NX

C = Private consumption in an economy

G = Total sum of government spending

I = It is total spending of public businesses on capital

NX = It is total exports of nation minus total imports

GDP has great importance for the economy of every country because it is considered to measure the economic health of the country and standard of living. GDP serves as an important measure to gauge the productivity of a nation.

Gross Profit Margin

Gross profit margin is an important parameter to assess the financial health of the firm because it helps you to calculate the proportion of leftover money after calculating the cost of goods sold. It helps you to pay additional expenses for the business and enable you to save some amount for future. It can be calculated as:

COGS = Cost of Goods Sold

Although gross profit margin will not help you to exactly estimate the pricing strategy of the organization, it is still a good indicator to know about the financial health of the organization. Less gross profit margin reflects the inability of the organization to pay operational and other expenses.

Hard Selling

Hard selling is a marketing and sales practice that is used by forceful, direct and explicit sales message. It is a totally opposite approach to a soft sell technique. Hard selling is considered valuable to force a customer to purchase a good or service in short period of time instead of any evaluating more choices. It is a high-pressure technique and can be more persuasive to drive more sales.

Hard selling technique focuses on specific products and services for their instant sale. For instance, you want to sell a car via hard selling technique, it is important to check the availability of the specific model, the demand of the car and increases in the prices of the car.

Hire Purchase

Hire purchase is an important legal term that enables a buyer to take goods in installments that will be paid over a number of months. Hire Purchase is a U.K. originated term that is also recognized as "rent-to-own" in the United States. Hire purchase contracts to enable customers to lease their required goods and get ownership of these goods after making full payment according to the contract. It is a common tactic that is frequently used by businesses to increase their earnings by getting new equipment. A legally enforceable contract is usually made to secure the transaction for all involved parties.

Hyperinflation

It is tremendously hurried and uncontrollable inflation and under this condition, the prices of products increased hysterically. Hyperinflation can make inflation meaningless and under this situation, the currency of the country quickly losses its real value. In the meantime, the value of monetary items remains same with respect to one another. These economic items are related to the government expenses. Excessive increase in the money supply without any support of GDP growth can cause this situation. Imbalance supply and demand of money can devalue the currency of this country. In order to balance this situation, sellers increase their prices to avoid potential risk.

Imperfect Market

It is a market, where it is hard to collect actual facts and figures because the information is not rapidly divulged to all participants. There will be no correspondence between buyers and sellers. In simple words, it is a market where perfect information flow is not rigidly adhered to buyers and sellers. A perfect market is not a really doable goal but still, it is considered as a beneficial model. Currently, you can easily find an imperfect market even in the United States. The advance financial market of United States also has proven of price corruption, offensively dispersed information and other marketplace inefficiencies.

Import Duty

Customer authorities of a state impose this tax on the imports and some specific exports of the country to raise the revenue of the state. Tax is collected according to the value of goods, weight, dimensions, size and different other criteria of items. Import duty is also known as customs duty, import tariff and import taxes. Concerned authorities of each state establish the duty rates. For instance, import duty rates are settled by Congress in the United States. These rates are published in tariff schedule and different rates are applied to different countries according to the trade relations between both countries. Usually, a general rate is followed for normal trade relations but the authorities may develop special rates for their special friends.

Incentive Marketing

Incentive marketing is a formal method frequently used for the endorsement of specific actions and conduct by an explicit group of people during a definite period of time. Incentive marketing is famous for organizations to increase the motivation level of their employees to achieve their sales goals by attracting as well as retaining business customers. In incentive marketing, different motivational devices are used including premium, special price, bonus, incentives, pay for promotion etc. It is important to increase the motivation level of your employees for the sales promotion and profitability. Specially devised techniques are used to persuade potential customers to buy your business products and services.

Inflation

The unhealthy and excessive rise in prices over a period of time is known as inflation. During this situation, prices of the goods and services rise abnormally leading to the fall in purchasing power of consumers. It is the responsibility of the central bank of the country to control the severe inflation while reducing the excessive increase in prices. Usually, central banks of the countries try to sustain inflation rate at 2 to 3 percent, because it is considered healthy for the economy. The rise in inflation can decrease the purchasing power of money; therefore, it is important to control this situation on an immediate basis.

Inflection Point

It is a point to notice significant changes in the progress of a corporation, financial system, or geopolitical situation can be noticed. This point can be considered as turning points as one can notice dramatic positive or negative changes in the results. The progress of the company, industries, and economies can be constant every time; therefore, inflection point has great importance to know about the significant changes in business trends. An inflection point has a great impact on the progress of corporation because it can be the result of any current action or activity of the organization. Regular changes in business and current business trends can be measured by an inflection point.

Intangible Asset

Intangible assets cannot be touched with your hands because of their non-physical nature. It is an intellectual property of an organization such as patents, copyrights, trademarks, goodwill, brand name etc. Intangible assets can be classified according to their nature. One can buy or purchase intangible assets of other organization through a legal agreement. Intangible assets have no obvious value, but these may prove really valuable for the firm to use in critical situations. Brand recognition is one of the famous intangible assets that can increase the profitability of your firm. For instance, Pepsi is a famous company, and its brand name has great recognition all over the world.

Internal Equity

It is the perception of employees regarding their errands, rewards and work conditions in comparison with other employees in a similar position. Internal equity is an important term linked with different considerations of a worker regarding wages and workload. It is a common practice among workers to evaluate their current work situation to have an idea either their salaries and rewards are perfect according to their skills and duties. It helps an employee to evaluate his/her value within an organization. Internal equity is applied in those organizations where workers prefer to compare their total wages with their duties in contrast with other workers.

Involuntary Liquidation

It is a legally enforced situation in which the company has to stop its business because of inability to pay debts. Involuntary liquidation usually happens at the instigation of any member of the organization. It is important to pay a premium to the stockholders during this process. Liquidation may take place on a court order to wind-up business on the petition of any creditor of the organization. Involuntary liquidation is a legal proceeding for the bankruptcy of a business by creditors. Creditors of the business have right to request for involuntary liquidation to court after noticing the inability of the company to carry out business operations profitably.

Keyword Advertising

It is an important form of internet marketing in which specific phrases and keywords are used. The basic purpose of this type of advertising is to grab the interest of people toward your products and services according to their needs. Google's AdWords is one of the famous keyword advertising programs. Some advertisement is posted on the websites of Google to increase the visibility of a website on search engines. This type of advertising revolves around specific phrases and words. Pay per Link is a common form of keyword advertising. Keyword advertising is a famous but effective technique to make your business website successful.

Market Penetration Price

It is an important strategy that is used to get a dramatic increase in the volume of sales and market saturation of a new product. This approach is used to advertise your product at wide level by keeping the price of new product comparatively low. Market penetration price is an assumption based strategy in which price, demands and profit margin of a specific product is based on assumptions only. It is an important technique to grab the attention of customers toward your new products and services. Its correct application will help you to get desired results. You can easily increase your market share and sales volume with market penetration price.

Market Segmentation

Market segmentation is an important way to get enough market shares by targeting specific needs of the target market. It enables business organizations to target different categories of consumers to design their products and services according to them. Following three criteria are used for market segmentation:

- Homogeneity (Similar needs)
- Distinction (Unique needs)
- Reaction (Response from market)

For instance, an energy drink company may target players and students. Both are different groups and the company will surely receive a really different response to the advertisement. Market segmentation helps business organizations to create products according to the requirements and specific needs of their customers.

Mixed Economy

Private and public sectors both are an important part of the economy because both sectors have their own role in the development of the economy. Mix economy features a blend of sectors, a certain degree of monopoly, and defense infrastructure.

Mix economy is also famous as the dual economy because it reflects the characteristics of both economies. A mixed economy can have strong regulations of market economies or there may be the strong provision of public goods. Usually, private ownership is preferred as a mean of production. The market often bears dominance of profit-seeking enterprises and private organizations. Expansions in some mixed economies have been made for the expansion of public enterprise sectors.

Naked Debenture

Naked debentures are unsecured debentures because these are not backed by any security; therefore, these are also known as uncovered debentures. Usually, a debenture is designated with a security issued by the company therefore in United States debentures are famous as bonds. Debenture has floating charges and different other securities like a mortgage. Naked debentures are totally opposite to normal debentures because these debentures have nothing at their back. The bearer of the naked debenture will not get any additional benefit. There is no security in the form of interest or any other charge. No benefit is being associated with the naked debentures.

Nepotism

It is a common practice to favor your relatives, friends and dear fellows with your power by giving them some benefits like jobs, promotions, incentives etc. Favoritism is another name of nepotism, and this term is widely used in business and politics because, in both fields, relatives are granted regardless of merit. Catholic popes and bishops are the founders of this term. Business, politics, entertainment, game, and religion are some fields that are severely influenced by nepotism. Relatives and close friends are showered with rewards without any merit under the influence of power. Nepotism gives rise to corruption in business ventures.

Oligopoly

It is a situation under which a small group is controlling a particular market. It is quite similar to monopoly, but in monopoly, only one company takes the control of the whole market while in oligopoly, there must be at least two firms to control the market. Controllers of the market under oligopoly are known as oligopolists. A gas market can be a good example of an oligopoly because this market is controlled by small firms. Under oligopoly, reduction in competition leads to higher costs of products for consumers. It is important for each group to be aware of the decisions and activities of others for strategic planning.

Chapter 11 – A Guide for the Beginners to Advance Traders

Blockchain technology is heating up in previous several months. The cryptocurrency rises steeply from less than dollar 1,000 in the month of March to an all-time high on August 14 $4,440.

Investment in cryptocurrency is quite different than regular stock. Investment in a business requires you to buy shares of this company and own a small percentage of the company. The person who invests in Ethereum or Bitcoin receives digital tokens that serve numerous purposes. With the Bitcoin, you will get decentralized currency that will become partially anonymous. If you are investing in Ethereum, you will get a piece of power to run smart contracts and decentralized applications.

Trading cryptocurrencies require dedicated exchanges. Larger exchanges, such as Gemini, Bitfinex, Kraken, and GDAZ offer solid volume for the trading of cryptocurrencies through credit cards or bank transfers. Coinbase is a growing option for its built-in wallet and ease of use. The tradeoff via coinbase can be really expensive. Poloniex is another exchange that offers 80% cryptocurrencies to traders, but the catch is the point that you can utilize only Bitcoins or various other cryptocurrencies to fund all these trades.

Top Cryptocurrencies for Investment

There are numerous paths that a person can decide on the investment in cryptocurrencies, but some popular options are here.

- **Bitcoin:** The name of bitcoin is famous all over the financial world. The price of cryptocurrency has increased almost 8x in the previous year. Moreover, the unique design of Bitcoin confirmed that there are almost 21 million in existence and it is difficult to reach this number in terms of the match. It means the bitcoin is not subjected to inflation.

- **Ethereum:** It is another famous cryptocurrency. Its price has blasted above 3,000% in last year. This growth has no effect on its price because it is less than 1/10th of a Bitcoin, so it could be a good choice for investors who don't have resources.

- **Litecoin:** It has risen above 2000% in last year. The P2P digital currency acts in a harmonizing way to Bitcoin. With its comparatively low cost, it is a solid entry point for new investors of crypto.

- **Monero:** It can be considered for its 2nd level of privacy other than Bitcoin offers. The price blasted in 2016 and cap of market amplified from 5 million dollars to 182 million dollars. The reason is the major adoption of cryptocurrency by darknet market "AlphaBay". The AlphaBay was shut down in July 2017 by law enforcement.

- **Bitcoin Cash:** In 2017 August, the blockchain Bitcoin spun off a nimble iteration known as Bitcoin Cash. It is similar to Bitcoin but has the important distinction that has capacity of extra block sizes. Price of this cryptocurrency is doubled from $300 to $6,00+. If you are owning a Bitcoin before the split, you will receive an equal amount of cash (Bitcoin cash). Almost 16.5 million units are available that make Bitcoin Cash the 3rd more valuable currency in the market and world. Its market cap is more than $10 billion.

- **Ripple:** It is a protocol that permits near the instantaneous settlement of transaction and decreases transaction fees to meager cents. Some VCs along with a few major banks (BBVA, UBS, and Bank of America) have executed Ripple in their systems. The main difference of Ripple from Bitcoin is that it is pre-mined and centralized.

- **ZCash:** It operates similarly to Monero. The cost of this cryptocurrency swelled in 2017 June to almost $400 but has leveled off to sub-$300 range.

Tips to Invest in Blockchain Technology

The blockchain powers Bitcoin and all other cryptocurrencies, but there are numerous ways to invest in blockchain tech without pour money into digital currencies. You can look at the startups of the blockchain.

Crowdfunding platforms are another option because blockchain startups often look in crowdfunding for success in their business in the infancy. The BnkToTheFuture is a platform that allows investors to invest their money in blockchain and Bitcoin startups. You can invest your money in ICOs (Initial Coin Offerings) of new projects of the blockchain. The blockchain organizations issue tokens or cryptocurrencies through ICOs to raise capital. This route is riskier because this form of crowdfunding is new, but the return is better than others.

Top Blockchain Companies and Stocks to Invest

The following six blockchain companies and stocks can be famous investment choices for you.

BTCS

With $7 million market cap and shares around 14 cents, BTCS can be an excellent entry point for the investors of the blockchain. It is the first public blockchain-centric company in the United States. They were one of the first entrants in this digital space.

DigitalX

It is developed by a particular mobile product known as AirPocket that helps with secure cross-border payment from 30,000+ locations in 14+ countries, especially in South and North America.

Global Arena Holding

This company acquires patent relevant to the blockchain tech, but it is working on the application of tech to ATMs. If they become successful, this would be a major application for regular customers.

BLT Group

This Vancouver-based organization offers solutions of blockchain across different spaces, such as fantasy sports and banking.

First Bitcoin Capital

This organization focuses on obtaining Bitcoin startups and financing them for the development of software and hardware cryptocurrency.

Concilium Group

The London-based company invests in other startups of blockchain to help in their development. It was the first renowned IPO for a tech blockchain company.

Chapter 12 – Strategies to Secure Information and Data with Blockchain

Data security is not an afterthought or luxury because there are numerous things to secure your data. Everyone can store his/her sensitive, personal and private information online. Nowadays, data is becoming the most valuable resource in this world. Market capitalization is dominated by numerous data-centric companies, such as Amazon, Apple, Microsoft, Alphabet, and Facebook. Keep it in mind that your sensitive data is becoming the main target for cybercriminals.

You may consider your data protected, but it may not be as protected as you consider it. Even massive companies like Home Depot, Target Corp, and Anthem had data breaches over a few years and this breach is affecting millions of customers. In short, current arrangements are not sufficient to keep your data safe.

Cloud services can't be the best solution because their centralized systems are becoming valuable targets. You have to trust a third party to store your important and sensitive data. In this situation, the current solutions are not sufficient so you should have something new and reliable.

Blockchain Can be an Alternative

Blockchain technology can be a major breakthrough of this era. The first application of Blockchain is Bitcoin and it allows a safe network of consumers to perform transactions without trusting anyone on a network, or even a 3rd party. Everything is securely encrypted and no one can tamper with Blockchain without coming into the eyes of everyone.

Bitcoin is deeply penetrated into your daily life and has a remarkable effect on investment, earning asset and payment. Nowadays, the ecosystem of cryptocurrency is innovative enough to allow users to practically get it with one click of a button. There are numerous cryptocurrency exchanges, such as CEX.IO that offers a wider range of trading, selling and buying tools to users. You can simply store your altcoins and Bitcoins on this platform.

Data Storage and Blockchain

There are different ways to use a blockchain to distribute storage software. The most common way is:

- Break up your data into small chunks
- Encrypt this data so that only you can access it
- Distribute the files of data over a network to secure all files. You can access your complete data even when the network is down.

Basically, instead of passing your files to an organization like Microsoft or Amazon, you can easily distribute it across one network of people all around the world. The cloud software is shared by a community and nobody can tamper or read the sensitive data of another person. This service is good for public services to keep public data safe, decentralized and available.

A cryptographic signature allows you to save a file or document on a Blockchain. This may give a way to users to ensure that the files are untampered without saving the whole file on Blockchain. When you access a file, you will get a guarantee to see the similar version of your document.

Smart contract is also useful to use with Blockchain. These ensure a particular transaction after meeting particular conditions, such as the records may be programmed to be updated or changed automatically.

Benefits of Blockchain Data Storage

There are numerous benefits of using cloud storage of Blockchain, such as:

- P2P networks may increase the speed of downloads, just like torrenting
- Your data will be distributed to all across the world so you can access it anywhere without any restriction
- There is no need to worry about a third person having access to your data
- It can be really cheap because you have to pay $2 for each TB per month
- You can rent out your free space and earn actual money.
- With a huge network with lots of reliable contributors, clever techniques will be useless and their redundancy factor is lower than 1.5.
- The blockchain records have immutable nature that means you will come to know about an unaltered and accurate file.

Possible Limitations with Blockchain Storage

Along with some benefits, there are some limitations and challenges of the blockchain.

Security is only limited by the network size. If the network of blockchain is not well distributed or large, it may become vulnerable to numerous attacks.

Increase in redundancy can be required than other models of storage if the network is not reliable or big enough.

Overhead network communication may be huge. This trouble is for engineers because they largely determine the viability of a technology. There should be a balance between security, speed, and usability.

The bandwidth of a network can be a huge problem as you can notice this problem with Bitcoin. With a maximum of 7 transactions in a second, Bitcoin is becoming more expensive and slower to use.

Current Storage Products by Blockchain

Blockchain technology is in development stages. There are a few organizations having some great ideas, such as Sia.tech and Storj.io are storage products of Blockchain. These are some early examples of development in this technology. Filecoin is also a product that makes mining easy with storage space. Filecoins may be traded for the storage space on this network.

Healthcare data may be an excellent fit for the Blockchain technology. The companies struggle with keeping the data of patient secure, auditable, accessible and up-to-date with all parties. In short, blockchain technology is expected to disrupt numerous industries. The secure market for data storage can be a revolutionary step to decrease the dominance of 3rd parties.

Chapter 13 – Docker is Useful for Blockchain App Developments: Learn about Docker and Blockchain

Docker is basically an open source and anyone can subsidize to Docker and expand it to your own needs. If you need additional features and these are not available, you can add them in the Docker. This tool is good for system administrators and developers. It is an important part of DevOps (developers and operations) tool chains. Developers can pay attention on the writing code without thinking about system that it may ultimately be run on. It enables them to get one head start with the use of thousands of predesigned programs to run in the Docker container. The operations staff can reduce the requirements of systems and increase their flexibility and productivity. It is a good way to reduce your overhead and footprint.

Getting Started with Docker

There are some helpful resources to get started with Docker to maintain your workflow. You will get one web-based tutorial along with one command-line simulator. It will help you to try basic commands of Docker and understand it's working.

Security and Docker

Docker increase the security of all applications running in the shared environment, but the containers may not be an alternate of security measures. You have to understand the security features of Docker to keep your containers secure. Basically Docker has three important elements, such as:

- Docker Images
- Docker Containers
- Dockerfiles

As one project, Docker offers a complete set of high-quality tools to transfer everything to make one application across machines and systems, physical or virtual, and brings loads of benefits with it.

Docker achieves full-bodied application and process and reserve containment via Containers of Linux, such as Kernel features and namespaces. The further capabilities may come from different components and parts of one project that extract the intricacy of working along with the low-level tools and APIs of Linux. These are used for the application and system management with regards to the secure containing procedures.

Main Parts of Docker Project

Project of Docker consists of different main elements and parts that all are designed on the top of existing functionality, frameworks and libraries offered by Linux Kernel or any third party, such as aufs, mapper or LXC.

Basic Parts of Docker

- Daemon of Docker is used to manage LXC (docker) containers on its current host.

- CLI of docker is used to communicate and give command to docker daemon.

- Image index of docker is a private or public repository for the images of docker.

Elements of Docker

- Containers of docker are directors with everything about your application.

- Images of docker are snapshots of base OS (for instance, Ubuntu) or containers.

- Dockerfiles are scripts to automate the building procedure of images.

Elements of Docker

These elements are utilized by these applications making the project of the docker:

Docker Containers

This whole method of porting submissions with the use of docker depends on the container's shipment. These containers are directories that may pack (tar-archive) like others. It can share and run crossways various platforms (hosts) and machines. You have to dependent on the host to run these containers. You have to install docker for this procedure. Containers are obtained through LXC (Linux Containers).

Linux Containers (LXC)

You can define these containers as an amalgamation of different Kernel-level features. It enables you to manage your applications and have their own environment. With the use of certain features, such as chroots, namespaces, SELinux and cgroups profiles, the LXC may contain application procedure and help with the management through restricted resources. It may not allow you to reach beyond your file-system and restrict access to the namespace of parent.

With containers, the docker makes it easy to use LXC and brings much more benefits along.

Docker Containers

The containers of docker have various main features and these features enable you to get the advantage of:

- Isolating procedure
- Application portability
- Prevent any assuaging with the external source
- Management of resource consumption

As compared to traditional virtual-machines, they require fewer resources for the deployment of isolated applications.

You are not allowed for:

- Messing with remaining procedures
- Dependency hell may be caused
- May not work on the different system
- You may be vulnerable to abuse and attacks to all resources of the system

Being depending and based on the LXC, makes one technical aspect and these containers are similar to directory, but one formatted and shaped one. This may increase the portability and gradually construct containers.

Every container may layer like one onion and every action may be taken within one container comprises of putting a separate block that actually translated to the simple change within your file system on the top of previous one. Various configurations and tools make this set-up effective in a melodious manner altogether (e.g. file-system).

This method will make containers extremely beneficial for you because you can easily create and launch new images and containers. These are kept lightweight because of layered and gradual procedure. Everything required a file-system and take performing roll-backs and snapshots in particular times. You can get the advantage of VCS (version-control systems). Docker containers initiate from the docker image that make the base of various other layers and applications.

Docker Images

These images establish the foundation of docker container and it is a point when everything just starts to form. These are similar to the default disk images of operating system that are utilized to run different applications on desktop computers and servers.

These images will help you to get the advantage of seamless movability across systems. You can make consistent, dependable and solid base with each and everything. It is required to run all applications. With self-contained options, the risks of system-level modifications or updates may be eliminated and the container turns out to be immune for the external exposure. This immune is important to prevent the hell dependency.

Some extra layers of applications and tools are added on the top of this base and the new images may be designed with the help of committed changes. A new container may be created from saved things and images to continue this procedure. The file system (union-file-system) brings every layer together as one single entity and you may work with one container.

These foundation images may explicitly state the working with CLI docker to directly form one new container and they may be specified in one Dockerfile to automate image building.

Dockerfiles

These are scripts with a series of consecutive instructions, commands and directions that can be executed to make one new docker image. Every executed command is translated to one new layer of onion and makes the end product. They can replace the procedure of undertaking everything repeatedly and manually. A Dockerfile may finish its execution and you may make one image to start one new container.

Chapter 14 – How can Docker help blockchain developers to improve data storage?

To effectively use your storage device, you should learn how docker creates and stores different images. You have to understand that these images will be utilized by containers. You should have short introduction to this technology to enable container and image operations.

Layers and Images

Every docker image mentions one list of layers (read-only) that represent the differences n filesystem. The layers may stack on the top of every other to make one base of one root filesystem of the container. The below diagram will help you to understand the image layers of Ubunto 15.04:

91e54dfb1179	0 B
d74508fb6632	1.895 KB
c22013c84729	194.5 KB
d3a1f33e8a5a	188.1 MB
ubuntu:15.04	

Image

Storage driver of docker is liable to stack these layers and provide one single incorporated view.

As you create one new container, you can add one new, writable and thin layer on the top of original stack. This layer may be known as container layer and all changes in your running container, such as new file writing, modification of existing files, removing files will be written on the thin layer of container. You can see the diagram to understand this procedure.

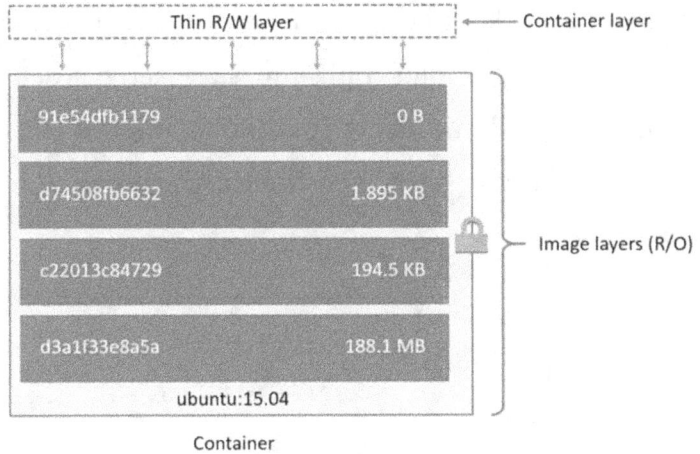

Container
(based on ubuntu:15.04 image)

Addressable Storage for Content

The 1.10 docker is introduced with one addressable model for storage. This is a new method to work layer and mage data on your disk. The layer and image data was stored and referenced with the use of UUID (randomly generated). In the unique model, you can replace it by one content hash.

This new model is good to enhance the security and offer one built-in method to avoid the collisions of ID and guarantee the integrity of data after push, load, pull and save activities. It helps you to share layers by sharing images even from a different built. See the diagram below to understand this:

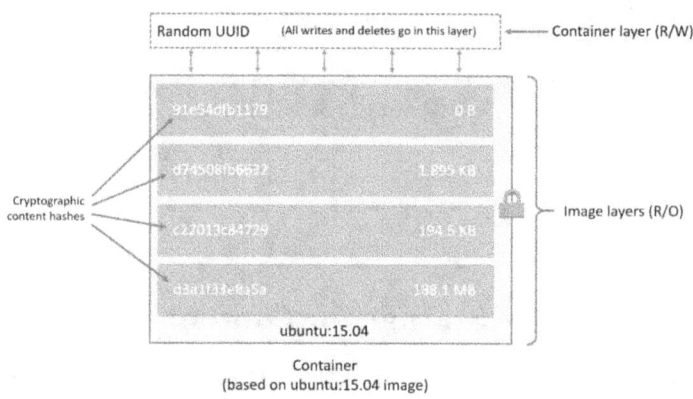

Container
(based on ubuntu:15.04 image)

You can see that all layers in the IDs are cryptographic botches and the ID container is a random UUID. There are various things to note in your new model, such as:

- Migrate current images
- Layer and image filesystem structures

Current images, pulled and created by the initial docker's versions, should be migrated before their use with the novel model. Migration may involve calculation of checksums and it is automatically performed for the first time while you start update of your docker daemon. Once the migration is finished, all tags and images will become new and secure IDs.

This migration procedure is transparent and automatic and it is intensive on a computational level. It means you have to take some time with image data. During migration time, the docker daemon may not give proper response to requests.

You can get the advantage of migration tool to migrate current images to new format before upgrading your daemon docker. The upgraded daemons docker will not have to perform the in-band migration and avoid any linked downtime. It offers one way to physically migrate current images to distribute them to other deamons docker in current environment with recent docker's version.

This tool is offered by Docker and it work as one container. You can use https://github.com/docker /v1.10-migrator/releases to download it.

If you are running migrator image, you have to expose the data of directory's host to your container. If you have to use default data path of docker, the command for docker can be this one:

```
$ sudo docker run --rm -v /var/lib/docker:/var/lib/docker docker/v1.10-migrator
```

If you want to use devicemapper driver for storage, you have to write --privileged choices to give access to storage driver to your container.

Example of Migration

Check the example below to use the migration tool on docker 1.9.1 version and AUFs drivers for storage. This host may run on one t2.micro AWS EC2 along with 8GB SSD volume, 1GB RAM and

1 vCPU. The data directory (/var/lib/docker) of docker consumed almost 2GB space.

```
$ docker images

REPOSITORY          TAG             IMAGE ID        CREATED         SIZE
jenkins             latest          285c9f0f9d3d    17 hours ago    708.5 MB
mysql               latest          d39c3fa09ced    9 days ago      360.3 MB
mongo               latest          a74137af4532    13 days ago     317.4 MB
postgres            latest          9aae83d4127f    13 days ago     270.7 MB
redis               latest          8bccd73928d9    2 weeks ago     151.3 MB
centos              latest          c8a648134623    4 weeks ago     196.6 MB
ubuntu              15.04           c8be1ac8145a    7 weeks ago     131.3 MB

$ sudo du -hs /var/lib/docker

2.0G    /var/lib/docker

$ time docker run --rm -v /var/lib/docker:/var/lib/docker docker/v1.10-migrator

Unable to find image 'docker/v1.10-migrator:latest' locally
latest: Pulling from docker/v1.10-migrator
ed1f33c5883d: Pull complete
b3ca410aa2c1: Pull complete
2b9c6ed9099e: Pull complete
dce7e318b173: Pull complete
Digest: sha256:bd2b245d5d22dd94ec4a8417a9b81bb5e90b171031c6e216484db3fe300c2097
Status: Downloaded newer image for docker/v1.10-migrator:latest
time="2016-01-27T12:31:06Z" level=debug msg="Assembling tar data for 01e70da302a553ba13485ad020a0d7
7dbb47575a31c4f48221137bb08f45878d from /var/lib/docker/aufs/diff/01e70da302a553ba13485ad020a0d77db
b47575a31c4f48221137bb08f45878d"
time="2016-01-27T12:31:06Z" level=debug msg="Assembling tar data for 07ac220aeeef9febf1ac16a9d1a4ef
f7ef3c8cbf5ed0be6b6f4c35952ed7920d from /var/lib/docker/aufs/diff/07ac220aeeef9febf1ac16a9d1a4eff7e
f3c8cbf5ed0be6b6f4c35952ed7920d"
<snip>
time="2016-01-27T12:32:00Z" level=debug msg="layer dbacfa057b30b1feaf15937c28bd8ca0d6c634fc311ccc35
bd8d56d017595d5b took 10.80 seconds"

real    0m59.583s
user    0m0.046s
sys     0m0.008s
```

With the help of time Unix command, the docker can produce time for a particular operation. If you want to migrate seven images taking 2GB space on your disk, it will take almost one minute. This may include the time required to pull the docker/v1.10-migrator image in almost 3.5

seconds. This similar operation on the m4.10 by large EC2 with 160GB RAM, 8GB EBS and provisioned IOPS and 40 vCPUs may take different time. See below to improve this operation:

```
real     0m9.871s
user     0m0.094s
sys      0m0.021s
```

It is enough to see the effect of hardware spec on the migration operation.

Layers and Containers

The basic different between one image and one container is writable layer on the top. All writes to your container may add one new or modify prevailing data stored in the writable layer. If you delete your container, it will also delete your writable layer. There will be no changes in the original image.

Every container contains its individual writable and thin layer and all changes will be secured in the layer of container. It means multiple containers can share the accessibility to the similar image and have their own state of data. See the diagram of multiple containers:

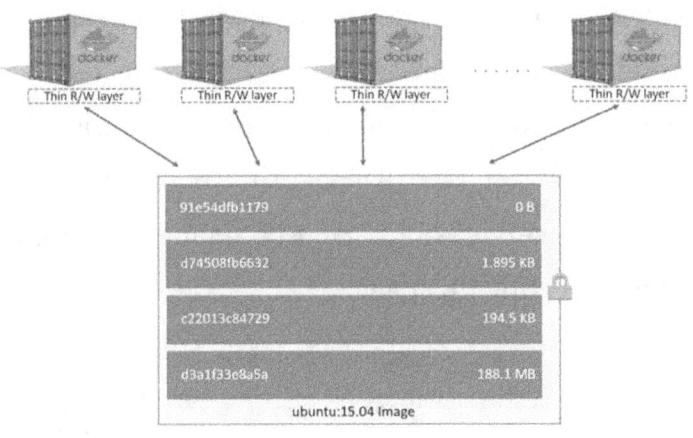

The storage drive in the docker is responsible to manage and enable both writable layers of container and image layers. The storage driver can accomplish between drives in a different way. There are 2 main technologies behind the container management and image of docker. The docker layer stackable images with CoW (copy-on-write) ability.

Strategy of Copy-on-Write

You can optimize resources by sharing them and people often do this impulsively in their life. For instance, Joseph and Jane are twins taking calculus classes at separate times from separate teachers. They can share their exercise book by passing it to each other. Jane has to complete the homework on the 11th page his book. Now, the original exercise book can't be changed and only Jane can copy this page.

Copy-on-write strategy is simple for copying and sharing. This strategy enables system (that requires similar data) processes the data instead of getting their own copy. At a particular point, if one procedure requires some modification to write data, only the procedure that should be written will copy the data. All other procedures will be continuing to the use of actual data.

Docker requires one copy-on-write technology with containers and image. This strategy can optimize the performance of your container and disk space. In the next section, the system will work to leverage the copy with containers and images via copying and sharing.

Promote Small Images via Sharing

You have to look at the CoW and image layers technology. All images have layers in the local storage of docker and managed by the driver of storage. The Linux-based docker may host this under /var/lib/docker/. These clients often report the images layers and the below command will prove helpful for you:

```
$ docker pull ubuntu:15.04

15.04: Pulling from library/ubuntu
1ba8ac955b97: Pull complete
f157c4e5ede7: Pull complete
0b7e98f84c4c: Pull complete
a3ed95caeb02: Pull complete
Digest: sha256:5e279a9df07990286cce22e1b0f5b0490629ca6d187698746ae5e28e604a640e
Status: Downloaded newer image for ubuntu:15.04
```

You can notice output because these commands can actually grab four image layers. Every line is listing the layer images and UUID has. Combination of these layers will help you to make your favorite images.

Every layer will be stored in the directory in the host of docker. It may use local storage area. Earlier versions of docker were storing every layer in one direction with similar name as the actual name of image layer. If you are using 1.9.1 version of docker, you can apply this command and get desired results. See the instruction below:

```
$ docker pull ubuntu:15.04

15.04: Pulling from library/ubuntu
47984b517ca9: Pull complete
df6e891a3ea9: Pull complete
e65155041eed: Pull complete
c8be1ac8145a: Pull complete
Digest: sha256:5e279a9df07990286cce22e1b0f5b0490629ca6d187698746ae5e28e604a640e
Status: Downloaded newer image for ubuntu:15.04

$ ls /var/lib/docker/aufs/layers

47984b517ca9ca0312aced5c9698753ffa964c2015f2a5f18e5efa9848cf30e2
c8be1ac8145a6e59a55667f573883749ad66eaeef92b4df17e5ea1260e2d7356
df6e891a3ea9cdce2a388a2cf1b1711629557454fd120abd5be6d32329a0e0ac
e65155041eed7ec58dea78d90286048055ca75d41ea893c7246e794389ecf203
```

Check the matching procedure of four directories with IDs layer of downloaded images. You can compare with similar operations perfumed on the host version 1.10 of docker.

```
$ docker pull ubuntu:15.04
15.04: Pulling from library/ubuntu
1ba8ac955b97: Pull complete
f157c4e5ede7: Pull complete
0b7e98f84c4c: Pull complete
a3ed95caeb02: Pull complete
Digest: sha256:5e279a9df07990286cce22e1b0f5b0490629ca6d187698746ae5e28e604a640e
Status: Downloaded newer image for ubuntu:15.04

$ ls /var/lib/docker/aufs/layers/
1d6674ff835b10f76e354806e16b950f91a191d3b471236609ab13a930275e24
5dbb0cbe0148cf447b9464a358c1587be586058d9a4c9ce079320265e2bb94e7
bef7199f2ed8e86fa4ada1309cfad3089e0542fec8894690529e4c04a7ca2d73
ebf814eccfe98f2704660ca1d844e4348db3b5ccc637eb905d4818fbfb00a06a
```

You can see matchup procedure of all four directories with the layer IDs of images.

You can notice different among image management in afore and after versions. All docker's version enables images to carefully share the layers. For instance, you can grab one image to share some similar layers of image as one image and it may be already pulled. The daemon Docker can recognize this and pulls the required layers out of their stored location. The second pull proves helpful to pull images with common features and layers.

This illustration can help you, just start with 15.04 Ubuntu image that you have recently pulled and make some changes into it to build a new image. You can use docker build or dockerfile command to make your work easy.

Take empty directory and create one simple dockerfile to start with 15.04 ubuntu image.

```
FROM ubuntu:15.04
```

You can add one new file and it will be known as new files in the /tmp directory of images and with a line "Hello World". Once you have done with it, the dockerfile will have these two lines:

```
FROM ubuntu:15.04

RUN echo "Hello world" > /tmp/newfile
```

You have to close and save file and from the terminal in similar folder as Dockerfile, you can run the given commands:

```
$ docker build -t changed-ubuntu .

Sending build context to Docker daemon 2.048 kB
Step 1 : FROM ubuntu:15.04
 ---> 3f7bcee56709
Step 2 : RUN echo "Hello world" > /tmp/newfile
 ---> Running in d14acd6fad4e
 ---> 94e6b7d2c720
Removing intermediate container d14acd6fad4e
Successfully built 94e6b7d2c720
```

Note: The (.) period is available at the end of above command and this period is important. It will communicate with docker-build command to utilize the current directory and build the context.

The above shown output will show you the new image and its ID will be 94e6b7d2c720.

Execute the docker-images command to authenticate the changed-unbuntu image in the local storage area of docker host.

```
REPOSITORY        TAG      IMAGE ID        CREATED          SIZE
changed-ubuntu    latest   03b964f68d06    33 seconds ago   131.4 MB
ubuntu            15.04    013f3d01d247    6 weeks ago      131.3 MB
```

You have to run the history of docker command to check the layers of images used to create changed-unbuntu pictures.

```
$ docker history changed-ubuntu
IMAGE            CREATED         CREATED BY                                          SIZ
E        COMMENT
94e6b7d2c720     2 minutes ago   /bin/sh -c echo "Hello world" > /tmp/newfile        12 B

3f7bcee56709     6 weeks ago     /bin/sh -c #(nop) CMD ["/bin/bash"]                 0 B

<missing>        6 weeks ago     /bin/sh -c sed -i 's/^#\s*\(deb.*universe\)$/        1.87
9 kB
<missing>        6 weeks ago     /bin/sh -c echo '#!/bin/sh' > /usr/sbin/polic       701
B
<missing>        6 weeks ago     /bin/sh -c #(nop) ADD file:8e4943cd86e9b2cu13        131.
3 MB
```

The history of docker output reveals the new image 94e6b7d2c720 layer at top. This new layer of image is easy to add because it is created by the tmp/newfile of hello world in the dockerfile. The four image layers under it are accurately similar image layers to make Ubuntu: 15.04 pictures.

Note: under the addressable storage content model familiarized with 1.10 docker and history data of image will not be stored in the configuration file with every image layer. It is stored as one string of text in the single configuration to whole image. This may result in the similar image layer and it will be shown mixing in the docker-history output command. This behavior is normal and you can ignore it. These types of images are commonly known as level images.

You can check the changed-ubuntu image because it doesn't have an individual copy of each layer. You can see in the below diagram that the image is shared with four layers with 15.04 ubuntu image:

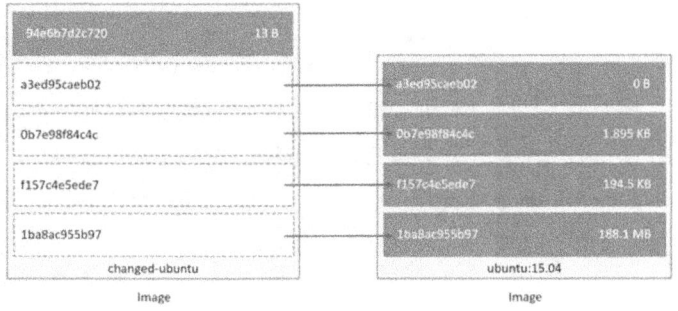

The docker-history command will display the size of every layer of image. You can notice the 94e6b7d2c720 layer consumes only 12 byes space on the disk. It means that the image of changed-ubuntu requires only 12 bytes extra space on the docker. All layers already exist on the host docker and shared by various other images.

Sharing image layers make the images of containers and docker really space efficient.

Copying can Make the Containers Efficient

Container is one docker image with one thin writable and layer of container. This diagram will help you to understand the layers of container on the basis of 15.04 ubuntu image:

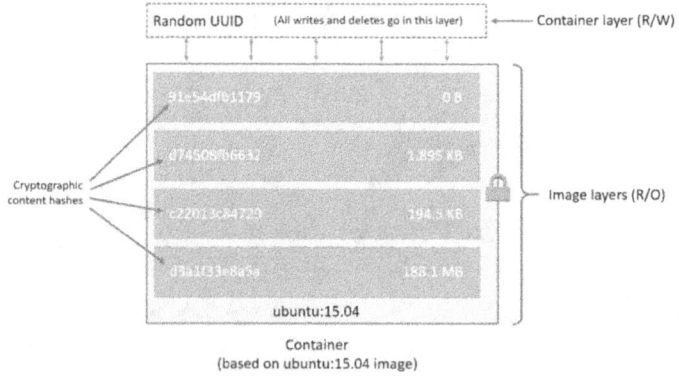

Container
(based on ubuntu:15.04 image)

All writes on the container are secured in one writable layer of container. The other layers are only RO (read only) layers and you can't change them. You can use multiple containers to share one single foundation image. The diagram below will help you to understand the sharing of images by multiple containers. Every container may possess its individual layers. See the image:

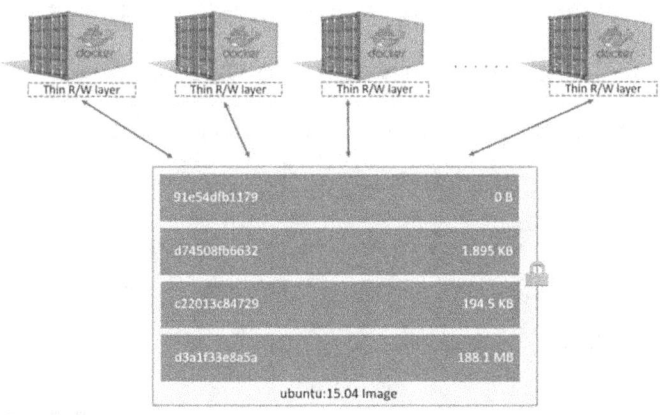

As you modify the existing file in a container, the docker utilizes your storage driver to perform operation of CoW. This may specify the operations on the basis of storage driver. For

OverlayFS and AUFS storage drivers, the CoW operations can be as follows:

- You can search through the layers of image to update file. This procedure starts at the top of your new layer and work in the downward direction to the foundation layer. It will work on one layer at a time.

- You can perform one "copy-up" operation on initial copy of your file. The copy up may copy your file up to the individual container with thin and writable layer.

- You can modify the copy of file in thin writable layer of your container.

ZFS, Btrfs and many other drivers can handle the CoW (copy-on-write) contrarily.

Storage Drive and Data Volumes

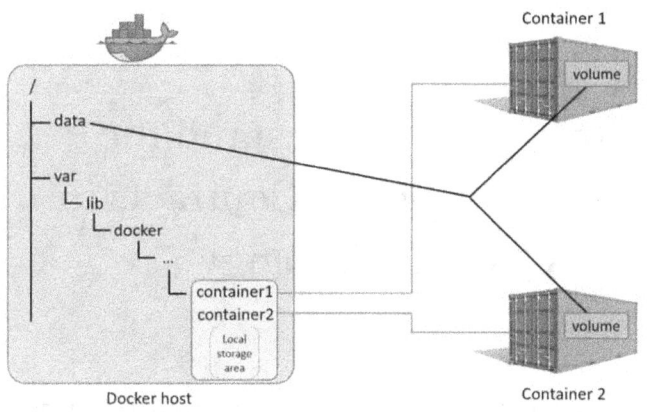

As you delete one container, the data written to this container may not be stored in the data volume is also deleted with this container. The data volume is one file or directory in the filesystem mounted directly in one container. These volumes will not be controlled by any storage driver.

Data volumes live exterior of local storage on the host docker. It can reinforce the independence from the control of storage driver. As one container is deleted, the data stored in the volumes persists on the host docker.

Chapter 15 – Understand the Concept of Smart Contracts in Blockchain Technology

The smart contract is a particular term used to describe codes of a computer program. It is capable to execute, enforce and facilitate the performance or negotiation of an agreement (contract) with the use of blockchain technology. The whole process is computerized and acts as a substitute or complement for legal contracts, where this term is recorded in the computer language as a set of particular instructions. Smart contracts offer a reliable method to issue tracking ownership of particular digital representation of value. Smart contracts are computer programmed and act as an agreement where the agreement terms are preprogrammed with the capability to self-enforce and self-execute itself.

Smart contracts aim to enable two anonymous parties to do business and trade with each other, typically over the internet without requiring a middleman. The history and origin of smart contracts are older than cryptocurrency bitcoin. This term was initially coined by alleged creators of Bitcoin "Nick Szabo" in 1993.

Smart Vs. Traditional Contracts

The contracts in the future will be similar to a hybrid paper-plus-code model where the blockchain is required to verify the authenticity of smart contracts. The paper backups should be filed to use as traditional resources.

Traditional Contracts

Traditional contracts, such as created by legal professionals contain legal language on printed documents. These contracts completely rely on the 3rd party for enforcement. This enforcement can be ambiguous and time-consuming. If things go awry, the contract parties have to rely on the public judiciary to solve this situation. This procedure can be time-consuming and costly.

Smart Contracts

These contracts are created by computer programmers through tools of contract development. These are digital contracts and written with the use of programming languages, such as Java, Python, Go and C++. The code defines the consequences and rules in a similar way as a traditional contract, stating the penalties, benefits, and obligations. These things may vary to all parties in different circumstances. These codes can be automatically executed via a distributed ledger system.

Conclusion

Blockchain technology has the capability to optimize the universal infrastructure to deal with universal issues in a particular space. Nowadays, everyone is talking about blockchain because this concept has keyed up a commotion in the financial industry.

The blockchain is considered as a public ledger of all bitcoin transactions that have ever been performed. One block is an important part of blockchain to record some or all current transactions and after completion, these all go into the blockchain as a permanent database.

Bitcoin is a ground-breaking payment network and a unique kind of money. It uses peer-to-peer technology to operate with central banks and other financial authorities, manages transactions and bitcoins are issued collectively by a network. This currency is an open source and it is available to the public. Blockchains technologies are used to control and record the transaction of bitcoin.